Ya Gotta Laugh!

Colleen Ashby

Copyright Notice

Published by Footprints Publishing, May 2022

© All rights reserved by the author.

This book is copyright. Apart from any fair dealing for the purpose of private study, research, criticism or review, as permitted under the Copyright Act, no part may be reproduced by any process without written permission from the publisher.

The views expressed in this work are solely those of the author and do not necessarily reflect the views of the publisher and the publisher hereby disclaims any responsibility for them.

 A catalogue record for this book is available from the National Library of Australia

ISBN (sc): 978-0-6451627-9-0

ISBN (e): 978-0-6454869-0-2

Printed by: iPrintPlus

Praise for Colleen's memoir *I Can See Clearly Now*

I have relaxed this afternoon by reading from cover to cover – yes, the entire story of Colleen Ashby! Remarkable story, absorbing detail written with such honesty! It changes one's perceptions & expands one's feelings towards family support & understanding the importance of accepting these offers… Hello Colleen, congratulations on writing an excellent book. I found it hard to put down from the minute I started reading it a few days ago. You have such courage, strength, independence, willpower and zest for life.
– Julie

I Can See Clearly Now *is a must read book that I highly recommend everyone reads. When you read her book, it refreshes your outlook on life. Colleen Ashby has great energy, zest, and spirit. She has a positive 'can do' attitude and joy of life. Colleen has overcome enormous adversity and obstacles. She has faced her challenges with courage, strength, and resilience. I invite you to engage and interact with Colleen and listen carefully to her amazing story and the lessons she has learnt from them for your own life journey. She can see clearly now… and it is refreshing to witness her journey… deeply guided by her experiences and spiritual knowing.*
– Margie

Hi Colleen, I loved your book (read it all the weekend you gave it to me). So proud and envious of you making it actually happen and for sharing your story. What a story!!!! You are truly an inspiration.
– Michelle

I bought a few copies of I Can See Clearly Now *and circulated them around. Such amazing heartfelt responses. What an impact you've had on so many lives.*
– Tristan

When you lose sight of where you're going in life,

Ya Gotta Laugh!

Colleen Ashby

Cover Design and Illustrations by Zoë Hoffman

Contents

Through the looking glass..	1
Waking up blind..	4
A relaxing bushwalk..	10
A walk along the beach...	13
Advantages of listening...	18
Named Quiche?...	21
Seeing eye dog 101...	23
But we need to stop here!..	29
Eyeing off the principal...	33
The rat maze..	36
Get it yourself next time...	41
I'm a champion too..	46
Flies? What flies?...	49
Free inbuilt GPS..	52
Going to the toilet..	57
Hey good looking, what you got cooking?...................	62
Hidden gems...	65
Keeping up appearances...	73
Learning from my mistakes...	78
Leaving a voice message...	83
Mystifying the children...	86
No rissoles...	89
Once you go black, you never go back........................	93
Playing battleships at dinner time....................................	96
Politically incorrect, but totally funny...............................	99
Power points and candles...	102
Raise your hand if you have a question...........................	105
Rockabilly rebel..	109
Total devotion or separation anxiety?.............................	117
Now just look at the camera...	122
Playing blind canasta...	126

It's all perspective..	130
Shopping in the perfume department.....................	132
Taking the final step..	136
Technology and apps...	139
Identity classification..	145
The biased and the unbiased..................................	149
Getting the lens right...	157
The blind leading the blind...................................	159
The warmth of a fireplace......................................	162
There is nothing wrong with my hearing................	165
Comparing the market...	169
Toothpaste...	172
Mistaken identity...	176
Playing the blind card..	182
Who is the patient?..	186
Lost in space... no, the bus port.............................	190
Book launch..	196
Don't drop the lead..	199
Parting ways..	204
Acknowledgements..	208
About the Author...	209

Introduction

Through the looking glass

January 2017, I had a heart transplant which went slightly pear-shaped. After four days in an induced coma with my chest cracked open while the medics did what they could to keep me alive, I woke up on day five with only five per cent of my sight. I am profoundly grateful for the gift of my new heart and, believe it or not, for having lost my vision. It has been a new journey to travel along and has completely shaped my world in a whole new way.

This book is my gift to you, sharing my experiences and insights through my new world as legally blind. My intention is to show that no matter what events happen to you in life, we all have the choice to decide how to deal with it. No matter what the traumatic event is at the time, when we look back, say five or so years later, it is often a pivotable point in life that has sent us on an amazing new journey.

At the beginning of any trek, quite often we regret taking that first step as we stumble and fall, but if we allow ourselves to fully experience the new surroundings and welcome them in, then the journey becomes so much more pleasant. Not only for you but everyone encompassed within your reach. Acceptance is a huge lesson for all of us to learn and it was certainly true for me. Even though at first, I thought I had accepted losing my sight, I discovered later that I was really fighting the inevitable changes that came along with it. I do feel now, though, I have come to a quiet surrender and have a lot more peace within me.

Stories in this book are my perspective and my personal thoughts or way of viewing things. There are some politically incorrect stories and if you feel you may be offended, then perhaps this is not the book for you. I tend to view life in a very non-serious way and try to laugh at things. I think people take life far too seriously and need to lighten up a bit. Let your imagination run wild occasionally and let your inner child out for a play.

I do not apologise to anyone who thinks my views or stories are offensive to anyone with a vision disability. This book is about me laughing at myself and nobody else. I express my annoyances and have my little rants but that is just life. We all do it, I am simply sharing mine with you.

My intention is to also give you insights into how someone with a vision defect does things in life. Not only informative but hopefully a good laugh at the same time. The stories don't have to be read in any order as they are all separate anecdotes occurring over the past five years. Just pick the book up and read a story at any time.

I have been gifted with not only my family; Les and sons Stephen, Mark and Scott, and my mum Pat, being able to laugh at the things that happen to me since losing my vision, but my dearest and closest friends also love to have a chuckle. It helps break the ice for other people around as well. So, if you ever come across a vision-impaired person, don't be afraid to say hello and have a light and open conversation with them. After all, we are just fellow travellers riding the high seas of life, and we occasionally need to look through the looking glass to find our direction again.

Colleen Ashby

Waking up blind

The thought of becoming blind is something no person would ever want to happen to them. That I can certainly guarantee. It would have to be one of the worst fears that one could have. For me, being a type one diabetic since childhood, it was something that had floated in and out of my mind through my life. Luckily for me, my eyes had fared well regarding this disease. I had always heard that diabetes is one of the biggest causes of blindness, so the reality of it occurring to me had always been a high possibility.

Like many eye diseases or conditions, the change is usually a gradual one, with time to adjust and learn new ways of doing things while sighted. This would still be a burdensome aspect to bare while waiting for the inevitable to happen. In some ways, I imagine this would even be worse; knowing that what sight you have now, will one day be gone. I am in many ways grateful that I never had to go through that process.

Waking up after four days from the induced coma after my heart transplant didn't go quite to plan, I was aware I couldn't see. Still weak from the surgery and disorientated with my surroundings, I really wasn't too sure of what was going on. I had been in a dream or, more correctly, a nightmare state for four days. Part of this dream included the image of a falling igloo over me, with black wavering movements that came in and out of focus. This is what my vision was now showing me, and I was confused as it resembled the dream. Initially the doctors thought it may just have been that my brain had been asleep for quite a while and needed time to readjust. With this in mind, it never really upset or bothered me. I was still very weak from the surgery.

As the days went on and my vision showed no signs of improving, to then be confirmed by the ophthalmologist that it would be permanently gone, it still didn't register to me as something to be upset over. Strange, I know. Any normal person, if that's the correct thing to say, would be extremely upset. That would be the expected response to have. Scared, angry, depressed would be anticipated, I am sure.

I classify myself as an eternal optimist, with a unique gift of finding the positive aspects which enable me to move forward in life. Accepting things for what they are and dealing with it. None of us have control over what happens to us in life, there are just too many external variables for this to happen. We do, however, have the power within us to choose how we are going to deal with it. There are always choices. We can be angry, frustrated, depressed with what has happened and decide to be like Eeyore with a rain cloud always hanging over his head, or we can accept the situation and work out a way to make the most out of life. I personally prefer to enjoy life with warm sunshine radiating down on me rather than rain. Give me rainbows and lollipops any day! People will also want to be around you if they have a chance of getting a lick of your lollipop. No one really wants to be miserable with a gloomy wet day.

I believe things happen to keep us on track for our soul's journey. I knew at a deep level that my life was meant to go in another direction. What that direction was, I had no idea. I also didn't want life to change for my boys or husband just because I had lost my sight. Determined to play the cards I had just been dealt, I needed to put on my poker face and get on with winning this game.

I remember my first drive home in our car. Les drove with Scott and Mark in the back. The only way that I could explain it to them, was it was like being on a ghost train ride. Everything in front of me was dark, like going through a tunnel with flashes of colours quickly whizzing past as we drove along. It was a strange sensation indeed as my brain was trying to work out what the pieces of imagery were.

One of the hardest things to come to terms with was the fact it wasn't a total blackout. I felt like a fraud. Classified as legally blind, but I could still make out colours and shapes. There were times when I lay in bed after waking and thought I had got my sight back as I gathered images of objects in my room, only to discover when I turned my head in another direction it disappeared. Other days I got panicky, feeling that my sight had deteriorated only to realise some time later it hadn't. My take on it is, my brain was still adjusting to its new normal and took a while to recalibrate the sensory input it was receiving.

Early on when I was trying to learn how to do things, the days were extremely long. Sitting and listening to the radio all day as that was all I knew how to do. Waiting for Les to return home from work for some company, some of those rain clouds certainly loomed over my head. I knew though that if I chose to let these clouds follow me around, life would become miserable for everyone, and I didn't want that.

I continually tried doing new things each day and improved on any skills I could. Things like walking down our back stairs, walking up and down our driveway and improving my fitness. I chose to keep on moving forward and soon gathered great momentum.

Yes, I certainly got frustrated and upset when I couldn't figure out how to do something, but I got over it pretty quickly. Leaving it behind and focussing on something else for the moment was the only way to stay on top of things.

One strange thing that still occurs is at night, when it is pitch black, it seems like there are lights on in the room. I even ask Les at times, 'Are there any lights shining?' But he will always say 'No.' That is a weird feeling, thinking that I can see things in the room when I can't. Try and work that one out! Another adjustment I wasn't expecting was the responses people had when they realised I was blind. To me, I was still the same old Colleen I had always been, and I didn't want that to change. Unfortunately, I came to realise not everyone knows how to deal with somebody who has obtained a 'disability.'

Close friends and family were great and treated me the same as always, but colleagues at work and people out in the public really struggled to make contact or conversation with me.

Some would give a bright hello as they passed me while others, I could tell, tried to sneak quietly and quickly past me, obviously not sure what to say or do. This certainly took me back a few steps in my self-esteem, feeling I was now somewhat alienated from the ordinary crowd.

I also thought I would be able to just slip back into the old familiar ways at work. Sitting around the staff table conversing and socially engaging with everyone. This did not happen at all. When you can't see the person who is talking, especially if there is other chatting going on, you have great difficulty in staying on track and it becomes quite stressful. Noise at any level is not tolerated so well either. I preferred sitting in my own office with Rhian, while the others continued socializing in the staff room.

While I was out in public places, I also became aware as time went on, that I was being stared at. Not that I could see, but whoever was with me would get cranky with the looks from people, who stared to the point of stopping and gawking as this bizarre show walked through. I felt like I was a bearded woman or like I had two heads! I have adjusted to this now, however, and it doesn't bother me anymore.

I can't speak for any other person who has suddenly lost their sight. I am sure everyone would behave differently and there is no right or wrong way. I am most probably not the best person to express their personal response since, as I said before, I have an exceptional ability to remain optimistic. I feel, though, by telling you of my behaviour, you might see that you can remain positive no matter what events happen to you. It really is a mindset and we can all train ourselves to focus our thoughts like this. It just takes commitment, time and a personal promise to live life in this manner. It guarantees life to flow with ease and joy, that's for sure.

Colleen Ashby

A relaxing bushwalk

There is nothing like going for a walk through the bush. Being one with nature, feeling the magnificence of the majestic, tall, empowering trees as they observe you going past. You can't do anything but feel lighter in your own being, breathing in the fresh air the trees emanate, listening to the bird's chirp calling out to one another. Mother Nature certainly has a way of bringing you back to the true source of life. Even if you are in a bad mood, a walk through nature will soon lift you to a happier state without you even realising it.

Up in the hills where I live, there are numerous bush tracks all throughout the local area. Many of these allow dogs to be off lead, so are ideal for giving Rhian a free run with our pet dog, Jasper. The dogs love getting out in the bush, smelling every waft of scent drifting through the air, having the freedom to run ahead and investigate rustles and noises. It's also a time for Les and I to just be together with no distractions. We all get a chance to just be and forget about everything else going on in the world.

As you have most probably gathered, I am fiercely independent and find it difficult to ask for help. I want to prove I can do anything by myself and will go to great lengths to show it. There are some ramifications to being this way, which are usually harmful to my body. Les, familiar with my feisty, independent ways, has learned to let me do things by my own accord. Most of the time I like it that way, however, sometimes it comes back to bite me on the arse!

Les and I will be walking along the bush tracks, which are obviously not smooth or level. Often, rocks jolt out of the uneven terrain, along with fallen sticks or branches. Gumnuts that the birds have dropped all over the path also turn it into an ice-skating rink of rolling balls requiring one to have the balance and poise of a ballerina to just stay upright. Strolling along together, chatting, watching the dogs as they frolic ahead, I am left up to my own devices.

I sometimes stumble over rocks or mis-step and lurch forward. As the ground drops away, Les will announce, 'Hole there.' Yep. Thanks, dear, for telling me after the fact. A few nanoseconds earlier would have been helpful. At times, he wanders way ahead as he decides to travel along a billy goat path, narrow and with overgrown bushes. He turns around, sees me way back and asks why I am taking so long! Unbelievable, right? Clever move, dear, getting your blind wife to traverse mountain goat country with no support. Let's put a blindfold on you and see how well you'd fair. You can see I get a bit narky at times, but justifiably so, I feel. Not until I yell out in pain from a stick coming up to stab me in my leg will he then say, 'Oh yes! Look out for the stick. I can see you have found it.'

I do enjoy my independence, but I would appreciate Les telling me when hazards are imminent and about to cause me pain or bleeding, but nope. He just casually walks and chats, obviously forgetting that I can't see! Don't get me wrong. I love that he doesn't smother or fret over me, but I do get a bit cranky when I've got blood pouring from my bruised legs. It sort of takes away the purpose of going out for a nice relaxing bushwalk to forget about the day's concerns. When I pick him up on it, he counters, 'But you like your independence, dear.' Now, I can't argue with that, but surely there is a point.

Ya Gotta Laugh

A walk along the beach

Going to the beach is one of our favourite outings, not only for Les and I but for Rhian and Jasper. There is nothing like being one with Mother Nature in her finest form, the majestic blue ocean in all its expansiveness and wonder. The smell of fresh sea air, the wind blowing through your hair, the feel of soft, warm sand between your toes, the sound of the waves as they hit the shore. Most of the time, Les will come for a walk along the shore while we throw the frisbee for Rhian into the water. This is when she is in her highest state of absolute dog bliss. Jumping the waves and swimming out to retrieve the frisbee, frolicking and entertaining herself in a complete state of euphoria. Jasper, not so fond of the water but loving meeting and greeting all his fellow canine friends, will be in his equivalent doggy joy. Yes, we all love a trip to the seaside.

Arriving at the beach early, before it got too hot, Les laid out the beach mat with our things and sat down. He was feeling tired from his busy work week and said that he was quite content to just relax and watch the passers-by while I walked the dogs along the water's edge. So, off we went without much thought of anything except of enjoying the sun, water and fresh air. With not a care in the world and only a few people scattered along the beach, I was in my element wading through the water, throwing the frisbee for Rhian and staying connected with Jasper as he walked along side of me.

As we went further along the way, the number of dogs and, obviously, people seemed to increase quite rapidly. Now there were dogs meeting and greeting one another, balls being thrown in every direction, and as I threw Rhian's frisbee there were several dogs going after it as well. Just to let you know, Rhian always retrieved it first as she is an amazing swimmer and has no qualms about heading straight out into waves that put the other dogs off. She has even swum quickly up to another dog that was ahead of her, swam over the top of it and pushed it down under the water to swiftly retrieve her frisbee. The owner of the other dog expressing his displeasure about the event and all I could say was, 'Sorry, she really loves the water and her frisbee!'

Totally involved with this chaos of canines, children, people chatting and playing with their beloved pets, it was easy getting wrapped up in this joyous state. Returning my attention to Jasper, I couldn't find him. Not too worrying, as he tends to run off and get distracted by other dogs. I decided to turn back as I had no idea of the time and wanted Jasper to see me if he came back from his distraction. I was still throwing the frisbee for Rhian but being more cautious now not to throw it if I heard people in the water. I didn't want to hit anyone in the head with it! Les would quite often tell me not to throw the frisbee at a particular moment, as I would hit somebody if I did. Without him, I just had to wing it and hope for the best. Thankfully I never heard any yells of disgruntled people.

As I neared to where I thought I had started, I noticed this dog crouched down, as if to invite me to throw the frisbee for it. Rhian was now off playing with some other dogs so I thought I would throw the frisbee for this crouched dog. Casting it into the water, the dog quickly leapt up and swam out after it, only to turn back with no frisbee in its mouth. Great! Rhian finally returned, prancing around eagerly as if to say, 'Well, when are you going to throw the frisbee?' I put my hands up in the air and said, 'Where is it?' That was her queue to go fetch it. She swam around in desperate circles, then ran up and down the beach searching for it, until I told her to leave it.

Continuing the walk back, I began to think I should be back at the starting point. The issue now was there was a multitude of people sitting on the sand and I could only see shapes, and they all looked the same. A slight rise in apprehension now occurred. I had no phone on me to call Les. If he had fallen asleep or couldn't see me then how was I ever going to find him? I didn't know how far up I should continue to walk as I craned my neck to the left to use the tiny bit of vision in my right eye. All the shapes looked similar as this feeling of panic was now rising within me. At the same time, I was trying to keep my attention on Rhian, so she didn't get distracted by other dogs. Just to add to the escalation of this event, we had only been to this beach once before, so I was not particularly familiar with it.

I mean what was I to do? I was now in the midst of a very crowded beach. For all I knew, Les had fallen asleep, and I wouldn't even be able to explain to someone where we were positioned. Think about it! As I was running through all these scenarios in my head, I heard Les call out my name. Extremely relieved, I headed directly up the sand. Les shouting, 'No, to the left!' I changed my direction and he called out once more, 'I am over here.' When I finally reached him, I blurted out, 'Well, I did really good, dear. I've lost the frisbee and I've lost Jasper!' 'So, you want me to go for a bit of a walk?' he said in a rhetorical manner. As he stood up, he told me the phone had rung a few times while I was walking. I dismissed it as it was probably just Mum or Mark, and I could check it later. Les and I were now on a search and rescue mission, so we headed back down the beach.

In no time at all, Les found the frisbee. Mission one accomplished, and Rhian was now back in her doggy heaven. Les was on high alert scanning through the volume of assorted dogs scattered throughout the whole beach area. We continued well past the point of where I reached previously, just in case Jasper had been distracted and travelled further along. Eventually we reached a point where there were very few dogs, so we turned around and headed back. Les was still intently observing the dogs as we went. Getting closer to our starting point, a feeling of desperation came across both of us. 'What do we do with a lost dog at a busy dog beach? We couldn't leave without Jasper but how could we find him in this chaotic and crowded dog venue?

Back at our mat, Les was trying to process our next plan of attack. I told him I would check my phone. Yep! I should have checked it when he told me as there were two voice messages about Jasper being found running frantically around up in the carpark. Huge sigh of relief. We successfully accomplished the second part of our rescue mission. Jasper's poor little heart was beating rapidly and shaking as he was passed over to us, but at least we were all together once more.

I don't think I will endeavour to walk along the beach by myself again until I have figured out a safer plan for not losing both the dog and me. It seemed like such a simple and harmless idea at the time. Starting off without a care in the world and not much thought about anything. How rapidly the tables can turn. It goes to show, when you lose sight of where you're going, sometimes it means things can easily go wrong. So, a little forward planning may be a good idea!

Colleen Ashby

Advantages of listening

There are some real advantages of listening to things rather than reading them. You may ask, why is this so? When you read, your eyes scan ahead of the point you are looking at. It's how your brain functions to be able to make sense of the words as you read. This is how speed readers can do what they do. Scanning and picking up every couple of words to get the gist of the story. When you listen to words being read out, however, you only hear the word that is being pronounced. You can't scan forward and pick up words ahead of that sound. This certainly has its advantages.

When Les reads out the recipe card that comes in the box of bagged food, he tends to jump ahead in parts. Trying to get the recipe straight in my head, I will ask him where a certain ingredient goes. He will tell me that it doesn't go in anywhere. I will, patiently though frustrated at the same time, say to read it out again.

Disgruntled with this notion, he tells me he has already read it and it's not there. I stand my ground and ask him once more to read it. As he reads it aloud, I will yell out 'There!'

'Where?' he asks. 'It's not there.'

'Yes, it is, I just heard it!' I confirm. 'Read that part again,' I tell him. As he reads it and I hear the word, I stop him and point it out. Now he is very subdued and making some reason why he never saw it. I tell him my ears hear everything!

It is not only Les who does this, but anyone who is quickly scanning and mumbling while they read something. Even with mumbling, my ears can usually pick up letters or sounds that I know make a word. Once you hone your hearing ability, you quickly become very adept at making sense out of only a couple syllables. This drives Les and friends mad, as I quickly tap and swipe my phone, already understanding what Siri is about to announce. To them, it is just gobbledygook, and it drives them nuts hearing this nonsensical gabble. Then, when I magically open the thing I was searching for on the phone to show them, they shake their heads in bewilderment wondering how I can make sense out of all that noise.

A prime example of this is when I was getting my first book published. Having the edited copy to listen to as read by Siri, I picked up several mistakes. Making a note by voice on a memo, I rang my editor and told her where the mistakes were. She was extremely surprised that I had found any after she had gone over it several times. Making the corrections, she joked that she should hire me as her proof-reader. Or, more correctly, proof listener! This became a huge joke for her as she told friends a blind person corrected remaining spelling mistakes. Perhaps a blind proof-reader is not such a silly notion.

This, I reckon, proves listening is a far superior skill to have over reading. What do you think?

Ya Gotta Laugh

Named Quiche?

When I was in Melbourne getting my new companion seeing eye dog, there was a lovely staff member named Teish. In fact, all the staff there were lots of fun, pleasant and easy to have a good relationship with. I had Teish's mobile number, as we had frequent communication.

While I was there in the training centre, learning how to handle Rhian, my new seeing eye dog, I would have to text quite frequently.

One of the things you need to use on the phone is an accessibility app called Voice Over. This allows you to voice everything and have Siri read it back to you. However, Siri not only has a limited vocabulary but also tends to have a slight hearing impediment at times, selective I would even say. On one of these occasions, I announced, 'Hey Siri, message Teish.'

'What do you want say?' Siri politely responded. I stated the message, remembering to punctuate the sentence as I went along. Then Siri said, 'Your message to Teish says, "Hi Quiche, I just wanted to confirm the arrangements for tomorrow…"'

Now, if the message has been a long one, sometimes I just leave the mistakes in there and hope they can be deciphered. I can tell you now it takes quite some skill to learn the mystical language of Siri, but it can be accomplished with dedication and tenacity. I would rank it up there along with learning Latin.

Next minute, Teish called me in raptures of laughter saying that she loved the new name Siri gave her! 'I've been called lots of things,' she said, 'but Quiche is the best one.'

I was trying to apologise while blaming Siri for the mistake, but Teish still laughing said she wanted to keep it. As we were both now joking around the comical name, we somehow came up with 'Cheesy Quiche.' Yes, that was it! Teish's full title would now be Teish Cheesy Quiche. From that point on, when she messaged or called me, she would say, 'Hi, it's Cheesy Quiche here.' If I gave her a call, I would even take it one cheeky step further and say, 'Hi Cheesy, how are you going?' It has become a fond and uniquely distinct way of greeting her.

Now, I personally think if you can make light and fun out of a situation that could otherwise be found insulting or be taken personally as a slant against you, a long-standing friendship can be made. It can also become a conversation starter to laugh about later. We all need to take life lightly and see the funny side to it. It certainly makes the world a more joyous place to live.

Ya Gotta Laugh

Seeing eye dog 101

My intention for this chapter is to fill you in on some questions you may have about a guide dog or seeing eye dog (SED). I will try to give you as much information as I can to satisfy your curiosity.

You may be asking, what is the difference between a guide dog and a seeing eye dog? The answer is quite simple. Two different companies with the same product. Comparable to choosing a Holden over a Ford. VisAbility train guide dogs, while Vision Australia train seeing eye dogs. It is just a personal preference with which one you choose. Like the saying goes: 'Same, same, but different.'

I feel the first topic or cab off the rank is toileting. When these dogs are trained, a strict kibble diet is a regime that needs to be rigorously adhered to. The simple reason for this is to control the timing of toileting. Another old saying: 'What goes up must come down.' Well, the same equation occurs, but this is more like 'what goes in must come out!' A measured amount of food at the same time every morning and night will generally guarantee a routine toileting time.

These dogs are trained to go out to the toilet on their lead to do their jobs. A toilet harness is placed around the dog's hind quarters with a doggie bag clipped to it. When you take them out on lead, they do it on command. Unclip the bag, tie it up and voila! It's all neatly done.

They are also trained to go to the toilet before leaving on any outings. This significantly reduces the need for toileting when you are out. If they do need to go, usually for a wee, then you need to take the harness off, as they are taught not to go while wearing it.

So, you can understand why a strict diet and no snacks are allowed, as it can throw the whole routine out the window. Not only that, but the dog must maintain a healthy weight to stay active and in good wellbeing.

When the harness is on and the handle is up, the dog is leading. When the handle is lowered, this is the signal for the dog to stop, sort of like a park brake. Handle up, drive. Handle down, park. Simple, right? Handle down also means that you are now taking over the driving skills and the dog just follows. This is a more suitable position if you are with somebody in an extremely crowded place. Way too hard for the dog to maneuverer, so holding the persons arm and being led with the dog following is much easier.

When Rhian travels on the plane with me, we are always allocated the front seat, where the baby basinets go. Rhian gets the window seat allocated to her. This has a wall and slightly larger leg room. Taking the harness off to allow maximum comfort, the lead is hooked around the window seatbelt. Always first on and last off to keep the boarding process flowing. Rhian travels extremely well, I just give her a nylon bone with some peanut butter on it after taking off and as we come into landing. This helps with any ear pressure adjustments that may occur. The meal directly before the flight is withheld so the need to do jobs is lessened.

Daily grooming is required. One, because they are working dogs, out in public places, so they need to be clean and look the part. This is done with a rubber brush with nobbles on it to massage the skin. Two, their undercoats need stimulating to activate the oil glands to keep their coat nice and shiny. Also, it raises any loose hair so it can be brushed out. This minimises having dog hair all over clothing, or dropping hair in places they go to.

If I am allowed to have a gripe, it would be when I am out with Rhian in harness and people have their dogs either off lead or on an extended one. Extremely frustrating when they think all dogs need to come and say hello and socialise. It's hard enough keeping a seeing eye dog focused away from dog distractions at the best of times, let alone when dogs come running right up wanting to interact! This really does make me want to release that demonic devil within me and it takes a huge amount of effort to withhold my wrath! So please, if you have a pet dog and ever come across any working dog, restrain your dog and let it go and socialise with the next canine that comes along.

Another gripe, to a lesser degree, is when people come up and ask if they can pat the dog. Whoever is with me will always speak up and say 'No,' along with 'Sorry, but she is working and can't be distracted.' I too will do the same thing. That's all right, at least they asked. What gets me annoyed, to say the least, is when they sneakily come up even after being told not too and pat her as we walk along! What is that? Really! Again, if you come across a working dog of any kind, please do not touch, talk, or engage with the dog. The simple fact is, while they are distracted with you, they have lost focus on where they are leading and will ultimately guide the person into an obstacle. They are there to do a job and not to interact with anyone who comes along. Sorry to be so brutal but sometimes it frustrates the hell out of me.

On a cheerier note, when Rhian is out of harness, she becomes just another dog. You can interact, pat and enjoy her all you like. She gets to socialise with lots of dogs at the beach and when she is having any free time. She really gets the best of both worlds. Traveling wherever I go and generally where no other dogs get to experience. Then she also gets to have her play time like any other normal dog. Now that, you would have to agree, is a pretty fantastic life.

Ya Gotta Laugh

But we need to stop here!

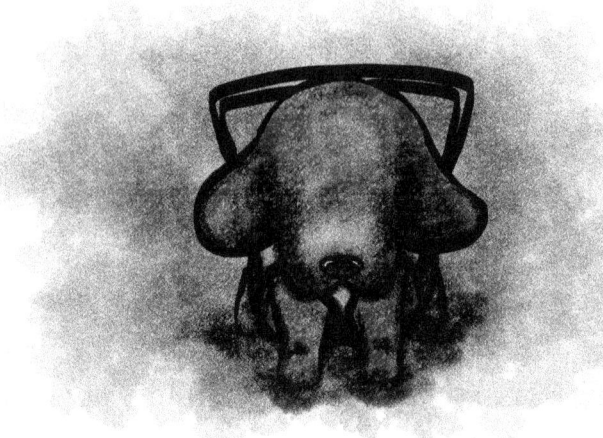

A seeing-eye dog, or SED as the blind community commonly calls them, is truly an amazingly well trained and extremely clever animal to have as your companion and guide in life. Not only do they learn a multitude of commands along with learning what to look for when asked to find something, but they also remember the places and routes you frequent. This is obviously important for them to be able to guide you to places that you often want or need to visit. Sometimes, however, they want to tell you where you need to go even if you don't want to go there!

In shopping centres I regularly visit, there are some shops I use frequently. Of course, most importantly when one is shopping, coffee shops are a must. Rhian, doing her important job, has naturally stored all these places in her large memory bank. She can very efficiently recall these items in an instant.

When you learn how to handle your SED, you learn never to tell them off for stopping somewhere you may have visited before, as they are merely doing their job. You just say, 'Good girl. Not today. Forward.' And then you proceed on your route. At times, though, Rhian is extraordinarily strong-willed when telling me we really need to stop here! Obviously, there are times I don't want to go where she's leading me, but she will have a different point of view.

I can be walking on the opposite side of the shopping centre to deliberately keep her from being near a certain shop's entrance, but she will be determined to weave her way through the crowd, pretending to guide me around obstacles and people, only to land right outside the shop I was wanting to avoid! A note to the reader: This shop is always where I buy her dog toys and when we do find our way to this section, she is like a little kid in the toy department. She noses through all the assorted colours and textures, sniffing and looking at everything. It certainly doesn't help when I pick them up to find out if they have those doggie attracting squeakers in them. This gets her extremely eager to see it go into the shopping basket. I guess I need to give her some allowance with wanting to take me into this particular shop, as she has a personal invested interest for what she may get from it.

Just recently I was at this shopping centre and needed to go right over to the opposite end from where we were. We were walking together at quite a reasonable pace, confidently making our way to our destination. Rhian skilfully manoeuvred her way around the people and obstacles in our path. As we neared my destination point, she suddenly stopped, turning her head to the left then back up to me. Realizing this was a coffee shop I regularly used, I said 'Good girl, not today, forward.'

Ready to set forth once again, I took one stride forward with Rhian before she planted herself, insistently turning her head to the left and then back up to me repeatedly, as if to say, 'We really need to stop here! This is where we always stop when we're out shopping.' She was standing steadfast and was not budging. I even dropped the handle of her harness. This is the signal that she is no longer leading but I am. Do you think she was going to budge? Nope, not on your nelly! Her head still pointed to the chairs and tables in the coffee shop. Out of the corner of my right eye I could vaguely see two male figures standing and waiting for their takeaway coffee, watching me. Now how embarrassing is this situation? Here is a blind person unable to get her seeing-eye dog to go where she wants it to!

Profusely scanning my brain for how to best handle this comical scenario, I came up with a plan of action. I bent down low to Rhian and said in a voice that was quiet but loud enough so that the two men could hear, along with anyone else entertained by this comedy sketch, 'Now, I know that we normally stop here and have coffee, Rhian, but we are going to stop at another place to have coffee after I have done my errands. So, we need to keep going and stop later on, all right?'

We both know there is no way a dog can understand all that conversation. Onlookers might have thought, 'Wow! How amazing is that dog, understanding a conversation like that?' Well, after having this heart-to-heart conversation with my bestie, I stood up and said, 'Okay, let's go. Forward.' And off she went, once again quite happily guiding me to my destination.

If I were an onlooker observing this amusing plight, I would be cracking up laughing on the inside. Animals have their own minds and idiosyncrasies we need to get to know as part of their interesting personalities. One of Rhian's quirks is not wanting to go out in the rain.

Let me tell you of another funny account regarding this. I was in Queensland on the Gold Coast and had just finished shopping downstairs in the supermarket. When I got back up outside, it was raining, and quite heavily too. When Rhian saw that the weather had changed not to her liking, she reluctantly moved out to where we needed to go but was keeping me well wedged against the side of the buildings to try and keep herself out of the rain. Needing to cross the wide-open mall, I waited until the rain lightened. When it seemed like more of a sprinkle, I gave Rhian the command to move forward. Hesitantly and with a displeased demeanour, she set forth. We made it to the other side and were back under the protection of the buildings' cover when she stopped, did a huge and somewhat over-exaggerated dog shake to dry herself, then looked up to me as if to say, 'Why did you make me walk in the rain? You know I don't like it!'

Just then, the skies opened up and torrential rain began. We ducked under cover of a building's walk-through and waited for a few minutes for the rain to cease, or at least lighten. When I thought we could make a run for it, I told Rhian, 'Forward,' but nothing happened! This was her first encounter with rain and I was a bit unsure of how to manage it. I tried again, 'Forward,' and still no co-operation. I dropped the handle and tried to lead her myself, but she just dug her haunches in and refused to budge one iota! All the while looking at me as if to say, 'What? You want me to go out into that? I don't think so!'

I was beginning to think I would be stuck there for quite some time. The rain showed no signs of letting up. What was I to do? I even got out my trusty dog treats to try and entice her forward, but she wasn't buying that little trick either. By now, I was having a conversation with her about how we need to get back and that there was some shelter from the buildings on the way home and that we needed to go.' To make this scene a bit more entertaining for you, I was surrounded by other people sheltering from the rain in the walk-through, and we were right outside an extremely bustling sports bar with people drinking and obviously watching this farcical situation. I was a bit embarrassed and quite frustrated over this circumstance. In a stern and commanding voice I pronounced, 'FORWARD!'

Rhian realised my nice happy tone had disappeared, heard this new serious, authoritative voice, then promptly moved forward. I normally don't like to use a harsh tone, but when I have run out of options for getting what I need done, I need to put away Mrs Nice Guy and bring out the big guns. Mind you, the guns don't stay out for long. Once we're moving along again, my praising voice returns along with a nice scratch on Rhian's back!

I have come to accept that, just like humans who have things we really don't enjoy doing, dogs being sentient animals too will have their own quirks and behaviours. They are certainly not robots and would be rather boring if they were. That bond you create together would be missing. I don't mind if she doesn't want to walk in the rain. I mean, I don't particularly like doing that either. Besides, she does so many other amazing things for me. She is an integral part of boosting my confidence and my positive mental state and I just love her to bits exactly as she is!

Ya Gotta Laugh

Eyeing off the principal

It was the end of term 4 at school and a staff gathering had been arranged to farewell the principal who was leaving. I had been absent all year from school, recovering from my heart transplant and learning how to do tasks of everyday living now I was blind. However, I really wanted to go to the farewell, as the principal had been tremendously supportive through my transplant journey. He told me he would have me back working in the school even he had to make me a new job role, so long as I wanted to return, of course. I wanted to thank him for all his support. I liked him because he was always approachable, funny and just simply pleasant.

A friend from school picked me up and took me over to the function. It was held outside in a lovely shaded, grassy area. There was staff and some long-time colleagues there to farewell him. Everyone was casually eating, drinking, exchanging conversations and laughter, along with shooing off flies! My bright, hot pink cane and I were led over to the principal, to say hello.

With a hearty and jovial voice, the principal welcomed me back. He was genuinely pleased to see me after all that had happened to me. Coming up close to him, I could see with the five per cent of peripheral vision in my right eye he had a blue suit and pale mauve shirt on. Leaning right in close, I moved my head up and down his torso to eye off his smart attire. As I was doing a very up-close and personal perusal, I expressed what lovely colours he was wearing. Then if that was not enough for him, I started running my hands over his well-tailored suit jacket across his shoulders. I commented on what a beautiful and well-made suit he had, along with how well it fitted him! To have a staff member come up, no doubt uncomfortably close, breaking all social etiquette rules, my face only centimetres away from his body, ogling intently, only to then have my hands run all over him like those of some half-crazed weirdo who has no personal space boundaries—if that wasn't enough for the principal, I don't know what is!

You'll be relieved to know I didn't take my appreciation even further by checking out his trousers. I think that would have definitely pushed the limit, even with the excuse of having basically no sight. There is only so much you can get away with by playing the blind card! I guess that could be used as an ice breaker in some situations, but I would have to choose them carefully. I don't think everyone would be so open and receptive as the principal was.

Ya Gotta Laugh

I still tend to go up to people, tilt my head to the left and eye off their clothing or jewellery if something catches the corner of my eye. It's not that I've developed some sort of strange fetish in getting extremely close to people and leaning right in on them, I'm just trying to see what I can by using the tiny bit of vision that I have.

The rat maze

I was on the Gold Coast for the Australian Transplant Games. I had travelled there a few days earlier with a girlfriend as my companion. Les, Scott and Mark were meeting me there later on. I had previously been on the Gold Coast earlier in the year so already had a comprehensive map in my head. The malls, shops, restaurants and tram stops that could get you from one end of town to the other were already imprinted on my frontal lobe cortex or whatever that part of the brain is called that does all that stuff!

There was one obstacle, however, I had to quickly overcome and that was how to find my way from the front of the resort up to my room. This was somewhat trickier than just a normal hotel as it had several towers and two entrances you could utilize. Personally, I prefer the one way in and out.

I had to learn to manoeuvre this rat maze proficiently within the next 36 hours because my girlfriend was flying down to Melbourne for the weekend to go to the football, returning to the Gold Coast on the Monday, so I would be here by myself. When we first picked up the keys and the receptionist gave us directions to our tower and then up to the room, I'm sure my friend looked the same way I felt. That feeling was, 'How the hell am I ever going to find my way?'

Suitcases in hand and Rhian by my side (hopefully taking in her new surroundings so we could find our way home), we set off down the rat run. Through the doors next to the internal elevators, follow the red line (there was a yellow line too), cross the underground carpark until you see the next set of double closed doors (where you needed to swipe your tag), enter through them, turn right until you reach another set of elevators, take the lift up to the fifth floor, once there go down the long corridor and the room is at the end. I hope you got all that because now you have to remember it all to backtrack to the front office. I hope you can imagine what was running through my head, especially after a long five-hour flight and then making our way to the hotel. In the midst of an overwhelming brain meltdown, I was in desperate need of a cup of tea.

Calming down over a nice hot cup of tea, we made a game plan to tackle the resort's cunning tactics in trying to bamboozle guests, especially blind ones. We would do practice runs several times over until both Rhian and I had mastered the resort's labyrinth, and this included learning how to come in from the other entrance. Determined and ready to be victorious over this challenge, we walked through both mazes over and over until I confidently had it down pat. I had no choice but to conquer this situation. Defeat would mean being stuck in the hotel room for the whole weekend, and that I certainly did not want!

Once I was finally feeling confident that I could find my way back to my temporary abode, both my friend and I were more relaxed about her flying to Melbourne in the morning. I personally felt very empowered and independent with the idea of being alone in unfamiliar surroundings. With no one to come to my rescue, I would have to work it out all by myself.

In the morning, I set off for the bright sunny day ahead. Beaming with enthusiasm and zest for this buzzing, vibrant metropolis, Rhian, and I walked down the pavement with our heads held high and proud. I stopped and ordered a coffee then went to find a seat, which Rhian does very proficiently, but I noticed it was extremely busy. Walking a few steps to try and sense where there were less people, I found a few vacant tables. It was considerably quieter here. I asked Rhian to find a seat, then, sitting down to enjoy the much lower drone of people chatting, I waited for my coffee. A waitress came over to tell me, however, that where I was sitting was a different coffee shop which was not open yet. She showed me to a vacant table in the right coffee shop, so I was now in the middle of a bustling and noisy cattle pen. The noises were like livestock being herded into a cattle truck and expressing displeasure about it. Sounds become muffled and hard to distinguish when you can't see where the projection is coming from. It is hard to explain, but you use your eyes to listen; to subconsciously lip read and watch facial expressions as cues to understand the context of

Ya Gotta Laugh

a conversation. So, there I sat, coffee in hand, listening to the mooing livestock in the middle of this metropolis cattle yard.

Still, I managed to fill in the day with a foot massage. A bit of self-pampering is always good for the soul. I met friends from the transplant group for lunch and had a very enjoyable day. Relaxing back at the hotel, Rhian had a chew on her bone with some peanut butter to destress and relax, and I felt a profoundly quiet inner sense. I could manage by myself if needed. It is an innate sense of survival that encompasses you. I'm not really sure how to express it.

I decided to heat my dinner up. I had brought it with me the day before with my friend, so all I needed to do was place it in the microwave. Without even thinking about this process, I went to push the button to start cooking. Then it dawned on me. I didn't know what button to press! I was pushing buttons left, right and centre. Do you think any one of them would make the damn thing work? Nope! I tried all variations of pressing buttons and not one of them would power up the device to give me a nice hot meal to eat. Disheartened and frustrated, to the point of tears, I reluctantly sat down and ate my cold meal.

I know you are most probably thinking in the big schemes of things, eating a cold meal is nothing to get worked up about and you are right. The issue is not the cold meal, it's the fact that simple everyday tasks usually done without thinking can soon become quite big obstacles with ways of slowly chipping away at your self-confidence and independence.

Once I get over the initial emotional distress and the all-encompassing anxious state of being, I can quickly settle down and put things back into well-deserved perspective. Yes, so I couldn't work out how to operate the microwave, but I managed to get around a new place, order coffee and sit down in the madding crowd like all the other people. I found my group of friends at a restaurant I hadn't been to before, and I mastered how to get up to my room all under my own steam. A cold dinner every now and then isn't such a catastrophe in the scheme of things. Sometimes we all need to just stop, slow down and review the situation we are in, to see it for what it really is.

Get it yourself next time

I had been on the Gold Coast five days when Les, Mark and Scott joined me. My family arrived late in the afternoon, tired after the long flight and just wanting to unpack, sit and relax. As I was confident with where everything was down in the mall, I offered to take orders for dinner and go down and get it. I needed to buy some groceries before ordering the men's preferred food. A large carry bag in hand, Rhian and I set off on our quest to hunt and gather food for the menfolk.

I walked with determination and pride. That I could carry out such a challenge by myself gave me a sense of empowerment. My first destination was the supermarket.

Knowing I had to go down the escalator, still beaming with confidence, I turned and continued walking in the direction of the supermarket. After what seemed like a slightly longer than usual time, I eventually came to the end of the building but found no supermarket. Realising my mistake, I did a sharp about turn and marched with a slightly quickened pace (so onlookers hopefully wouldn't notice that I didn't know where I was going) as I backtracked to the escalators. Continuing in the right direction, I soon came across my first destination. I grabbed a basket to put my items in and proceeded to go gather my groceries. Walking through the fruit and vegetable section, I could see bright green. I ventured closer to make out what fruit it was. Up close and running my hands over the fruit, I knew they were grapes. Deciding that they would be a refreshing and welcomed snack, I bagged some up and continued my shopping. I walked up and down the aisles until I came across boxes shaped as though they might contain tea bags. I could only see the bright blue, however, and couldn't read the labels. I heard some other people next to me in the aisle looking for items so I asked them if they would mind finding the box of tea that I wanted. Enthusiastically, they charged to my rescue and began looking, saying out loud what brands they saw. When they passed me the brand I was after, I could tell by the tone in their voices they were happy to be of service to someone in need. It doesn't hurt when there is a beautiful seeing eye dog by my side. Making the most of this convenient situation, I asked if they would mind searching for the jar of coffee I wanted. Once again, they jumped eagerly into good Samaritan mode and before I knew it, I had the coffee in my hand. Thanking them, I asked if they knew where the sugar was, they told me it was the next aisle over.

Strolling down the next aisle, I had no idea where the sugar was so had to try and find someone to help me. Luckily, there was someone coming up the aisle, so the same process began. Now I had the essentials, I proceeded to the checkout. Now, you must picture that this supermarket was in central downtown of a highly popular tourist spot and so extremely busy, especially as it was school holidays. Not really knowing where the checkouts were, I just followed the crowd with trolleys until I ventured across a self-serve checkout. Okay, I thought, I know how to scan items, which is a no-brainer. I felt like a rooster strutting his stuff, secretly proud that any onlookers may watch and wonder how a person who can't see can do shopping. Oh yeah, baby, I was internally beaming with assurance. Casually, I scanned my items and placed them in the bag. When I placed the bag of grapes onto the scanner, I realised I had to look up the item to be able to weigh it. A rapid panic rose inside of me, and a sense of embarrassment and gloom clouded my brain.

What was I to do now? It was extremely busy. I couldn't see any staff to help me. Did I just leave everything on the checkout and walk away, or did I try to pack it back into the basket and find a supported register? No, I couldn't walk away and leave the things here, as I needed them. Shit! Turning my head around into the empty vastness of noise and sensing impatient people wanting to get through the checkout, my fluffed-up rooster tail feathers had not only drooped right down; it felt like they had completely fallen out!

Just then, an assistant who obviously saw my distress asked if he could help me. 'Yes, can you weigh these grapes for me, please,' was my response. He asked if there was anything else he could help me with, and I scanned my mind to realise I wouldn't be able to choose the correct buttons to appoint the preferred payment method. 'Yes, can you select the payment method so I can pay, please?' Before I knew it, I was exiting the supermarket with all my goods in hand, and with a slow settling of my heightened emotional state. The next task at hand was to hunt and gather nourishment for the men. Tail feathers settling back in, a slight strut returned to my stride, I set forth on my quest.

Coming across the pizza and kebab shop, I stopped and asked what pizzas they had. Observing that I had Rhian, they began telling me all the items available. My brain was about to overload with too much information as I listened to the menu being rapidly read aloud. I stopped them mid-sentence and asked to just have a meat lovers pizza, please. Once I received the large pizza box and thanked them, I went to start off on the last leg of my journey. Now, to set the picture a little better for you, I need to add that it also had begun to rain. Not heavily, but wet all the same. My left arm was also taken up with Rhian's harness, while my right arm had a large carry bag with some heavy items, and now I had a large pizza box to carry! How was I going to carry the pizza, which needed to stay flat? I never went to finishing school for deportment, so carrying it on top of my head was out of the question. The only option was to place it sideways under my arm and hope for the best.

Eventually, I returned to the hotel from my arduous quest, all notions of self-empowerment and enthusiasm completely wilted like a dying weed. I pulled the box of pizza out from under my arm and threw it on the table, declaring that dinner was served. The men came over to sooth their ravenous stomachs, then opened the pizza box to find smashed pizza (like smashed avo, but not). Looking at the scrambled and unappetizing pizza, then up at me; wet, exasperated and obviously cranky; they knew not to say anything but a huge 'Thanks, Mum.' My only comment was, 'Next time you can get it yourself!'

This was a great lesson for me in my endeavour to be independent. Even though I knew I could do this whole task (and obviously I proved that it could be done), the amount of time, effort and obstacles to overcome are just not worth it. I prefer to go shopping with someone to help find the items and pay. The other fact is when you have a dog in harness, you are physically limited in what you can carry. I know I could do it if I had to, but I now choose not to!

I'm a champion too

Over on the Gold Coast at the Australian Transplant Games, I was poolside with Rhian and my family, anxiously waiting to compete in my events. It wasn't just the fact I would be swimming in a race which I hadn't done since I was eight years old, but I had also pledged on a television show that I would win gold at the Transplant Games. That pledge made in front of millions of viewers around Australia certainly added to the pressure of accomplishing the goal. I also had a set of cameras following me around all day.

It was time for the show to begin, with the fifty-metre freestyle. Standing on top of the block and waiting for the start gun to go off, the only thought running through my head was of hitting the wall first with a huge slap. *BANG!* The gun exploded and I pushed off the block with all my might, then just focused on powering through the water.

I slapped the wall and anxiously called out to whoever may be there, 'Did I win?' Being unable to see, I had no idea if I was first, last or somewhere in the middle. Then I heard my friend come over and exuberantly announce that I had won gold. She slapped my hand with a high five. My heart was pounding from the race. I was so elated with my achievement, and succeeding in completing my pledge. Yes, I could and did do it! Man, what a relief that was.

It came time for the place getters to receive their medals. Hearing my name called out, I proudly walked with Rhian over to the podium. I was beaming with pride as I was guided by a marshal up the step to the top platform. Rhian remained on the ground while I held her lead and told her to sit. The other two medal winners came and stood either side of me on the podium. Rhian, watched them come over and stand on the platform, she was curious about this whole procedure, what was it about. Then the medal giver came over, leaning forward to place the gold medal around my neck before moving onto the silver and bronze place getters.

By now, Rhian was totally confused as to her part to play. This was definitely not something that had been in her training and all she knew was, she had to be with me by my side to guide me. She was pacing in tight circles, looking up at me as if to say, 'I really need to be up there with you.' As we winners stood with medals around our necks to have our photos taken, it all became too much for poor Rhian.

Next thing I knew, she had done a flying leap up onto the winners' platform with me. Now these platforms do not have generous space for standing; in fact, there is only enough room for one set of feet. Definitely not space enough for a set of dog's paws as well! As Rhian took her mighty leap to get to me, she sent me flying backwards, knocking my legs so I lost my balance. Luckily, there was a marshall standing behind me, who gallantly saved the falling maiden from toppling out of the castle window. He managed to grab hold of me from behind and steady me back into place. Meanwhile, Rhian was quite happily standing on the podium where she knew she was meant to be.

I received a further three gold medals and a silver that day but decided against taking Rhian with me over to the podium again. I think staying with the family and watching me receive the medals was a much safer option.

Rhian's endeavour to be near me was the talk around the transplant community that night, resulting in a lot of laughter. I mean, here I am, up on the podium having received a gold medal, beaming with pride, when Rhian does her flying stunt. The crowd initially gasped as they see the inevitability of me falling backwards and potentially coming to some quite serious bodily harm. Only to be saved by a knight in shining armour. The onlooker's sense of trepidation turns into relieved laughter.

There I was, Rhian up on the platform with me, looking up as if to say, 'Well I'm a champion too!'

Ya Gotta Laugh

Flies? What flies?

We all know how annoying pesky flies buzzing around your face can be. Always having to do the Australian salute, as we Aussies call it. Swatting and shooing those annoying and relentless critters away from us. Then, if that's not bad enough, we are always trying to be watchful guardians keeping a close watch on the sacred food, to keep it from being contaminated by germ-infested invaders crawling all over it.

None of us like the thought of one of those bug-eyed pests buzzing down our throats if we accidently consumed one when taking a bite of a meal. Nor do we like the idea of one of those wretched things laying eggs on our food, contaminating it with their larvae. Silly, really, when you think about it, as it would just be another form of protein, but our minds run wild with a lifetime of being told how annoying and filthy these flying irritations are. I must admit, when they land and crawl over your skin, there is something ticklish and irritating about it. You just know it's an insect that should not be meandering all over your body.

Now, I still must put up with the annoying skin aspect of flies, along with hearing that incessant buzz they make as they zoom in and out of earshot, but I no longer need to be miffed with watching them land on my food. I don't get bothered by a need to swish those nasty little critters away. I don't see them, so it doesn't bother me. Great, I think! Everyone around me is always watching with laser-focused eyes ready to attack any oncoming invaders. They shoo off flies around my food as well as their own, while I just merrily get on with eating my meal. Now that's a really positive aspect to losing your sight, I feel. Don't you? If one did happen to land in my food and I ate it accidentally, I wouldn't know about it. What you don't see, won't hurt you. I bet you never thought about that advantage, did you?

When it comes to food, there is another real payoff when you lose your sight. If you can't see something, then you obviously can't get drawn into impulse cravings, at least not by the sight of food. You can still get drawn in by wafting aromas but seeing cakes in a cabinet or chocolates and lollies brightly wrapped on the shelf have no alluring power anymore. It's great because unless I really feel like eating something specific that I know from memory, impulse temptations lose their influence over me.

The same rule applies when you are at a buffet style meal. Someone will ask me what I would like to eat. My answer is,

'You will have to tell me what there is.' As they start looking over the food, saying the names of the culinary delights laid out before me, I'll say yes to the foods I like. However, sometimes they may skip or just skim over some of the tastier delights, and it is not until I hear someone else comment on how delicious something is that I ask if there is any of that food available. Of course, then they make a fuss apologising and put some on my plate quickly, as if they have been found out cheating. I suppose you could count that as a half-point loss, a disadvantage.

There is another downside to not being able to see things and that would come under the sub-heading of Occupational Health and Safety (OHS). I tend to forget about items in the fridge like jars of relish or salsa. As we all know, there is an expiry date to food items, but naturally when you can't read the date, it's not particularly helpful, is it? I will generally smell items before I use them but quite often things smell fresh because of the strong spices in them, when in fact there may be some furry bits of mould growing sneakily on the sides. Grated cheese is a killer for that and it's not until I'm sprinkling some all over the nachos that Scott will come along and notice the grey cheese instead of yellow. He has become particularly good at picking all the yucky bits off! If I'm not sure how long a jar of food has been in the fridge, I will, nine times out of ten, check with someone if it looks all right to use.

A note to the reader: No one has yet come down with salmonella poisoning or even had any bouts of gastro from my cooking, so I must be doing all right.

Colleen Ashby

Free inbuilt GPS

It is said when you lose one of your senses, the others will heighten to compensate. Well, I can tell you another sensory faculty that got exceedingly enhanced was my sense of direction. I must admit that I have always had an aptitude for knowing where places were when I travelled, but now, well, let's put it this way; I almost don't require google maps anymore. I seem to have developed my own inbuilt GPS in my brain.

Places where I have lived or frequented in Perth and regular holiday destinations are super easy to navigate. I can remember all the landmarks and signposts that give directions. If someone tells me what we are passing, I can tell them what's coming up next and where to go.

A friend was taking me to the hospital for a clinic appointment but hadn't been there before. I told her not to worry about putting on her navigating system as I could give her directions. Driving along, chatting at the same time, I would tell her when she had to exit onto another road. I would even explain what lane she needs to be in, what roundabouts or lights were coming up, along with the names of the roads. As we got to the point when she needed to enter the carpark, I could sense she was driving too fast for the turn. I expressed in quite a loud and slightly high-pitched voice that she needed to slow down as she had to turn right about where we already were. She said, 'so why didn't you tell me earlier?' and laughed. She was, and still is to this day, amazed.

I can also tell a driver who is following a navigating system that there is an easier or faster way of getting to where we are going. Sometimes when they think they know where something is and I say that they are wrong, they find it extremely hard trusting a blind person to show them the way. After they try their way and can't find the required destination, they will exasperatedly give in and allow me to point the way. Quiet astonishment and reluctant recantation are admitted. This is the part where I have great internal satisfaction, a huge smug Cheshire Cat grin on the inside, deeply wishing I could say, 'Believe me now?' I would never do that of course, as I wouldn't like the idea of making someone feel humiliated, even though at times it can become frustrating. Now when people seem lost but doubt I could know where to go, Les tells them to follow me as I do have this uncanny gift of mapping. A lot of the time he just relies on me to tell him where to go (and I mean that in a directional sense, not the vexing or infuriating manner).

When I travelled to Queensland and Sydney, places I hadn't been before, within a day or two I already had some sort of map running in my head. Told the landmarks, names of roads and any other information, I can quite easily know where we are or how to get to places. At times, I even amaze myself. It really is quite impressive, I feel!

It's comparable to being like Dustin Hoffman in *Rain Man* but instead of numbers scrambling through my neurons there are maps and names of places and roads. I think you would agree that having a free navigating system with you wherever you are, is an impressive tool. A very handy gift to be given since losing my sight. I don't think I could even try and lose myself if I tried!

Ya Gotta Laugh

Going to the toilet

Don't get all funny or weird with what this anecdote is about. It has absolutely nothing to do with the bodily function of relieving oneself. You definitely don't need sight to do that process. This is about when you need to utilise a public toilet. Not only finding the correct one but also finding your way out! Sounds a little bit silly, you may think. Well, after you read this, you may change your mind.

When I need to go to the restroom and I am with either Les or one of the boys, they don't like to venture to close to the toilet entrances. I don't know if they are concerned with what people may think of a man standing outside of a ladies' toilet or really just can't be bothered walking any further than they have to. I'm not sure. But inevitably, they stand some distance away and just point me in the general vicinity then expect me to somehow find it. Maybe men think women have some instinctual honing ability that directs us to the women's toilet, like it is an ancient ceremonial meeting place for women to congregate and share whispers. Again, I don't know. Some toilets in the bigger shopping centres have more of an open plan style, where you have a common entrance and then inside you have the choice of taking a left or right turn. It's almost like a maze, trying to find your way into the secret passageways that open into the restroom.

I know you are most probably thinking that there are visual and braille signs on these toilet entrances, and you would be absolutely correct. The issue is I can't see the figure of the little stick man or woman, nor have I learned braille. I generally hesitate before entering one of these passageways or doors that lead into the toilet. Hoping that someone will either open the door and confirm I am heading in the right direction, or, as on many an occasion, a voice from a stranger will say that is not the one I should be going into.

Once, I walked all the way into the restroom area, trying to find the doors to the cubicles only to stumble across a sequence of urinals! Quickly realizing my mistake, I hastily walked out, but not before I passed a gentleman walking in. I know I shouldn't feel embarrassed, as I really do have a good excuse for mistakenly being in there, but I still do. I could have said to the gentleman, 'Sorry, but the dog can't read signage very well!'

The other interesting aspect of going into the toilet cubicle, if it is not a disabled one, is size. Some of the new ones seem to have the same real estate issue as housing does now, and that would be cramming in as many as possible in a limited amount of space. You know what I mean, don't you? When you open the cubicle door, you need to gingerly scrape around it, so you don't knock the huge toilet roll dispenser. Then, as you lock the door and proceed to pull your pants down, quite often you will knock your arm on that oversized toilet roll apparatus anyway. I'm not exaggerating here, either; some toilets are ridiculously tiny. Well, now try and fit a dog in a harness in there! It takes quite some skill to be able to perform this manoeuvre, not only on my part but poor Rhian has to squish and position herself in there as well. Even more awkward is the reversing manoeuvre which requires an elite commanding skillset, to get us both out of there unscathed. It's almost like performing an SAS drill.

Due to what I have just explained to you about the size of the toilets, I usually prefer to use a disabled toilet. They are much roomier, better for when you have a dog with you. These, too, have their own set of issues for the visually impaired. Some of the new fancier ones have these push-button locking systems, with automatic sliding door closure. If you're standing too close to the door, it won't close. When it finally does close, and you go to push the lock button and hit the wrong one, it opens up again, and you have to patiently wait for it to do its thing before trying to get it to closed.

Once I have finished being bamboozled with trying to work out the secret combination of the locking system, I can get on with the task I had ventured into toilet for. After washing my hands and getting Rhian ready to set off once more, I sometimes have trouble finding the buttons again. Again, I am not making this up. One particular toilet I visited was huge. The buttons were close to the door but the toilet was right over on the other side, and then the wash basin was up the opposite end of the room, a good five meters away. I felt my way along the wall until I found the door and then continued even further along, eventually finding the panel of buttons. Relieved that I have found the magic portal out of here, I pushed the button. Nothing happened. I pushed it again, and still the door stayed shut! I was now beginning to get a wee bit panicked. I knew Les was outside somewhere, but this was at a movie theatre, noisy with the crowds of people in the foyer. He didn't have his phone on him to call. First lost, and now locked in the toilet, how was I going to get out? Like a lion trapped in a cage, I began frantically pushing anything I could feel around the button panel area. It seemed as if the magic portal button had some secret fingerprint required to obtain access and exit this Tardis. Finally, the Tardis decided to open its door and let me out.

Les came over and asked what took me so long, as we were waiting to go into the movies, so I explained my scary encounter with the disabled toilet Tardis! Even though it was definitely not funny at the time, we both had a great laugh about it after. I am particularly careful before entering any of these disabled toilets now, making sure whoever is with me tells me where the buttons are to lock and unlock, so I can get out of there.

You may also be asking yourself, why would someone who can't see what's up on the screen want to go to the movies? It certainly doesn't match up, going to watch something when you supposedly can't see, right? I'll let you in on a little secret. Movie theatres have provided a service called Audio Description. You have most probably begun hearing about it on television now that certain programs provide this service. Well, movie theatres do it too.

A few of the movies supply this facility. You are given a set of bluetooth headphones linked to that cinema. When you turn them on, audio describes what's being shown in the movie. When there is dialogue, you just listen to that, but when there is music and scenery or, say, a fight scene, it describes the characters and what they are doing. Les uses Audio Description all the time when we are watching Netflix now. He says it picks up details that are significant to the story that you quite often overlook when watching it. Audio Description also reads any subtitles shown in another language. This is one type of date I love doing with Les, especially as he quietly narrates the expression on people's faces as we ask for tickets end enter the theatre with Rhian. These are the little gems that make me sparkle; knowing people are bamboozled over this strange scenario!

When you see a blind person entering a cinema with their bag of popcorn, showing genuine interest in the program, now you know how they are doing it.

Colleen Ashby

Hey good looking, what you got cooking?

When I first began to try out my culinary skills again, there were, on quite a few occasions, some interesting dishes. I did not have any of the accessibility technology (AT) yet. These devices can read bar codes and tell you what the item is or read writing on items where you focus it. One setback, though, is they cannot read labels on cans. It needs to be a flat surface. So, I just had to go with what I thought things were by feel, or by the colours of their packaging. You would be quite surprised how similar some things feel when you can't see the label.

My very first solo attempt was when I realised how helpful your eyesight can be when doing things! My dish was a casserole, made in the slow cooker. I knew enough from all my years of cooking to not need a recipe. Some may call it winging it, I call it being experienced!

I had put in most of the ingredients already, except for a can of tomatoes. So I got the can of tomatoes out from the pantry, opened it up and poured it in, but nothing came out. I shook the can again, bewildered, and still nothing! How strange, I thought. I got a spoon to dig into the can and find out what was in it. It was solid. Spooning out a mouthful of the contents, I put it in my mouth. I spat it out quickly, into the bin. It was kidney beans. Not a delicacy I choose to consume by itself! I need to add in here too that I tried smelling the spoonful of ingredients prior to shoving it in my mouth but it did not have any odour I could smell. Still, I managed to complete the dish successfully, with a great critique from the family that night. Only the can of kidney beans was wasted. Not too bad for my first attempt, I feel.

Another time, I was baking a banana cake, which I had made quite regularly, so I knew the recipe by heart. I usually made it with both flour and almond meal, as this gave it a lovely texture and added to the taste. Putting all the ingredients into the bowl and beginning to mix, something seemed it was not right. I took the packet of almond meal over to Les to check it was just that. He simply said, 'No, it's breadcrumbs.'

'Oh well,' I sighed in slight disappointment, 'looks like you'll be having banana cake with breadcrumbs.'

The cake didn't turn out too bad in the end, the boys never even noticed the difference and the whole cake was devoured by the afternoon! In my defence, though, breadcrumbs and almond meal feel remarkably similar, and the packaging is also the same. Well, to a person who can't see, anyway!

The other extremely important part of executing a fine dining experience is serving it up. It not only has to look enticing, but it also needs to be evenly portioned out, especially when you have three men in the house. As I bet you are imagining by now, this too is a tricky task to perform. Serving up even amounts onto four plates is not accomplished without the help of someone's eyes. So, when at least one of the boys has been watching from the other side of the bench, usually highly amused at my attempts to evenly serve up, I ask if it looks even. No, would be the obvious response. They tell me what plate needs more of this and a little less of that. By now I'm feeling a wee bit agitated, and wanting to get the food on the table before it goes cold! Then I tell them, in a slightly exasperated tone, to come over and help me serve up. The same rule applies when I try cutting things into even slices or portions. It is never even, I can tell you.

Now, I don't even bother trying to dish up. I just call one of the boys to come and give me a hand to serve dinner. Between you and me, they enjoy watching me try to do impossible things. I guess at least I can keep them entertained, and have a laugh about it at the same time!

I have just returned after completing the following task I'm going to share with you. Only because, as I was doing it, I thought to myself, this really needs to go in the book. So here I am, back again.

Chicken and mayo rolls. Such a simple meal, but a favourite with most people (vegetarians excluded of course). Yep, simple to make and delicious to eat. Plus, the procedure is foolproof. Anyone can make it. Before I begin my telling of the process,

I must first set the scene. My kitchen benches are a light grey colour. The bread rolls are white and placed on the pine wood bread board, so it all begins to blend in very closely. Remember, the yummy moist flesh of the hearty chicken is white, and the crucial component to add flavour and moisture is garlic aioli or mayonnaise, both of which are white too. Getting the picture now?

After laying all the bread rolls open (pre-cut is preferred since, as previously mentioned, my cutting skills leave a lot to be desired), I begin to spread the mayonnaise over the tops and bottoms of the buns. This in itself is messy, as I can't see the difference between the bread and the mayo. I tend to put a lot on, too; I don't want the bread to be dry. Things are already beginning to get messy, and the mayo is now covering the knife down to the handle and all over my hand. It is quite remarkable how quickly and easily it manages to spread everywhere! I usually have to run my finger lightly over the bun to check it has been sufficiently covered. I then start spreading the broken or shredded chicken along each bun. Once more, after I have enough chicken on it, I need to feel if there are any patches of bread with no meat. Again, I tend to over fill the roll with chicken, worried I haven't placed enough on it. Time to enhance the chicken with a little seasoning. You know what is coming next, don't you? Obviously, I have absolutely no idea how much salt or pepper is coming out of the grinder (that goes for any spice). Most of the time, the food I prepare is laden with salt and quite often pepper as well. Then comes the finishing touch. There is nothing worse than having a dry chicken roll, so to make sure that doesn't occur, I give it one more good squirt or spread of the knife with mayo!

You won't need a vivid imagination so you can picture the MESS that is now all over the kitchen bench. Mayo is dripping down the sides of the rolls. Add in the smears over the board and bench with many lumps of chicken. My fingers are sloppy with mayo. I usually wash my hands frequently during this process, but some always manages to stick somewhere! Now I have to wrap the rolls up in plastic wrap, and even though I am extremely proficient at this part (as it is similar to putting on a baby's nappy), there is inevitably mayo on the outside of the wrapping, and God only knows where else!

Cleaning up is quite a task. Les usually intervenes if he is around. Once he sees me smearing chicken, mayo, salt and pepper over the bench, he gallantly steps in and deals with the mess.

The main reward of this very messy and simple task is the men always comment on how scrumptious and moist the rolls are, with plenty of chicken and mayo. That makes it all worthwhile, regardless of how sloppy the preparation is.

Hidden gems

Losing sight has revealed some wonderful hidden gems to me. These little beauties have made my life more stress-free, waking me up to a bright new world I have been slowly discovering. Some may seem trivial to you, but to me they have been a refreshing welcome. Let me tell you.

I used to be, not quite to the level of OCD, but extremely fastidious in some of my habits. One of these habits was keeping hair off my pillowcase. Every morning and evening, I would carefully look over both sides of my pillow. A detailed investigation, like that of Sherlock Holmes looking for clues in a murder mystery. Carefully I retrieved any of these creepy and infesting hairs from the place where I rest my delicate head. This used to annoy Les to pieces, as I pecked hairs off my pillow like a chicken pecking for worms. Well, now with no sight, I no longer get bothered with hair on my pillow. Now, you must agree that is a gem worth having, right?

I was also fastidious with dusting and wiping benches down all the time. Nope! Not anymore. Losing my sight has gifted me a miraculous dust-free house along with clean, shiny floors all the time too. Now, that would be something every woman would give anything to have, and I am the lucky one to have it. Almost as good as winning lotto!

I also, like most of the modern world, was addicted to social media. You know the ones I mean. Checking every five minutes to see if someone has posted some exciting news about what they had for lunch, or what they cooked for dinner, or even more importantly who they are socialising with. Most important to know this stuff going on in people's lives. I am guilty of taking part in this cult behaviour. Well now, due to Siri's deficiency in detailing the description of photos, I have drastically lost interest.

Don't get me wrong. Siri is most accommodating and extremely helpful in many other areas, but imagery is not one of her fortes. The most amount of detail goes something like this: A picture containing outdoors, sky and people. Great, that is immensely helpful Siri! Even better is when she tells me there is a coloured image containing text. Yep, right. Again, enormously helpful. NOT! So, with her significantly limited ability in this department, I don't spend much time on social media platforms.

I now prefer to be out in the real world with nature, listening to the sounds of birds and feeling connected to Mother

Earth instead of trying to listen to a description of nature on social media. That one is beyond being any kind of gem, it's like a diamond!

Speaking of the time-wasters in which I used to partake, there were also those addictive online games. I haven't played them for so long now, I couldn't tell you the up-to-date games. Back in the day, however, some of my favourites were candy crush and the various ones where you needed to grow crops and feed your farm animals, then save enough equity to build a shop and sell your wares. Man, what a time-saboteur that was, but you couldn't help yourself from doing it. I can't believe how many hours I wasted playing those useless games. Now, I fill my time listening to audio books, music and enjoying real-time life. I really don't miss the games at all.

When I first had to come to terms with not ever being able to drive again, and had to give up my car, that was a big adjustment I had to make. Especially where I live, where buses only run once an hour, so public transport is not the most viable option for getting around. The cost of a taxi, even with a discount, is still an expensive option too, and not one that I use at the drop of a hat.

Relying on friends and family to get me around initially got me frustrated, as I felt like my freedom and independence had been taken away. However, with time I have come to realise the gem in this scenario too. I no longer must pay all the running costs of a car. I have very nicely adjusted to being chauffeured around like in *Driving with Miss Daisy*. Sitting back, telling them where I want to go, listening to the music or catching up and chatting with a friend, no longer contending with all the other maniacs on the road. I reckon that one is ruby level. What do you think?

I now get to have menus read out to me when eating out. Now that's like being a member of the royal family. I imagine a butler coming over and running through the cuisine on offer, to then say, 'If that pleases Ma'am, then I shall have it prepared, thank you,' as he bows and steps back before retrieving my meal. This is the level of service I get when out anywhere. I have people running around after me, finding items I am looking for whilst shopping. Let me tell you of an encounter I had at Christmas time.

I had a list of what I wanted, so I told Mum to sit and have a rest on one of those lovely, comfy lounge seats some of the nice shopping centres provide. I told her I would be back in a jiffy, then Rhian and I set off. My first stop was the Nespresso shop. Standing in the middle of the shop, an assistant immediately came over and asked if I needed help. I gave her a list of all the items I wanted, and she ran around all over the shop, gathering my things while I just stood there with Rhian. Now with the items in my bag, I set off for my next checkpoint.

Coming across what I thought (but wasn't sure) was the retail store I wanted, I stood in the doorway and waited. An assistant came over and I was able to confirm this was the shop I needed. I told her exactly what I required, and she set out on her mission, swiftly returning with the goods. She led me up to the cashier counter to pay and I completed the transaction. Taking advantage of this good Samaritan who obviously still wanted to help the poor blind person as best as she could, I asked where the sunglasses shop was. Eager to be of service, she told me that she was more than happy to take me there.

Following her up through the arcade and around the corner. She triumphally escorted Rhian and I while keeping a close check on us to ensure we were following. She proudly handed me over to the sunglasses store and told them to look after me. I thanking her very kindly as she departed. I was now at my final destination.

Telling the new assistant what style of sunglasses I liked, she ran around and gathered several pairs. She was obviously bewildered as to how I was going to check out how the sunnies looked on me and was unsure as to whether she needed to bring me a mirror. I told her there comes a point, when you've lost your sight, where you have to trust people. Asking her which style suited me better, I soon had all the items on my shopping list.

I returned to Mum with a bag full of goodies. She was surprised I was back so soon. I told her I had first-class service all the way, and now we could have coffee. Now, that is what I am talking about; having royal service like that is definitely sapphire-status-worthy!

Another gem, or more correctly, an exquisite and expensive pink diamond as far as Les is concerned, is clothes shopping. As I have said before, I do like to look nice and I take pride in myself, especially so when I was working in the high school. Teenagers can be brutal at the best of times when talking about peers behind their backs, so God only knows what they say about the staff. I for one wasn't taking any chances with becoming a target! This, however, comes at a price. Well, that's what I told Les anyway!

I rather enjoyed online shopping, especially when you would receive this gorgeous glossy magazine with models showing of the fashion designs so beautifully. Who can resist that? Not me, I can tell you. Plus, it is so quick and easy, you don't even have to drive anywhere. It can be delivered to your front door within days.

I still receive the magazines but my enthusiasm for them has somewhat diminished. I still savour the process of opening the magazine and feeling the smooth glossy pages, but my viewing experience of the fashions has been severely lessened. Scott enquired one day as to what I was doing when he saw me holding the magazine up within one centimetre of my right eye and moving it up and down in my range of vision. I merely replied that I was clothes shopping! He just laughed and left me to it.

The significant value of this little diamond in the rough took me some time to understand but now I can honestly admit that I bought a lot of unnecessary clothes before losing my sight. I have completely turned the tables on fashion buying; if I don't need something, I won't buy it just because it looks pretty. I admit I wasted quite a sum of money on keeping up appearances. Now I see the value of this little hidden gem too.

My very first experience with people eager to be of service has left a long-lasting impression that I don't think I will ever be able to erase from my memory. I felt like I was in a Monty Python skit with John Cleese being the overly helpful assistant.

Ya Gotta Laugh

I only had my bright pink cane then, before the days of Rhian, but with this iconic blind symbol, I still caught people's awareness. Standing at the front of this computer shop, an assistant quickly came over to see how he could be of service. I explained what I needed the computer for, and he eagerly told me he could certainly assist me. With that, he went on to make the grandest and most exaggerated announcements as he carefully led me through the crowded shop.

Every few steps he would quite loudly tell people to move out of the way. Even those who were sitting on stools had to get up and make a wider gap for me to walk through. I felt as if I were some obscure and rare curiosity people go to see at one of those unbelievable circuses. The bearded lady and elephant man can go eat their hearts out compared to me!

Imagine John Cleese announcing in his authoritative comedic voice, 'MOVE, MOVE PLEASE, BLIND LADY COMING THROUGH! GET OUT OF THE WAY AND NO PHOTOS UNTIL YOU'VE PAID YOUR MONEY. QUICK, QUICK GET OUT OF THE LADY'S WAY!' All as people dive to the sides from where they stand and gawk in astonishment at this bizarre and never-before-seen act walking by.

If that wasn't bad enough, the assistant made a person sitting on a stool get off so I could sit down on it! I may be vision-impaired, but I'm not physically disabled! I must admit he was extremely obliging, setting my computer up with all the bells and whistles I required, along with showing me how to do some of the tasks. I am not making fun of him, as perhaps I was the first blind person he had ever assisted, and he was just being overly cautious with not wanting me to trip up on anything.

With a little practice, I am confident he could do it discreetly, with a bit less publicity! In fairness, though, I received far better and more thorough assistance from him than I have ever experienced in my life.

I hope I have shown you how losing sight has some real benefits. It has given me the opportunity to have a greater appreciation of real-time life. Being outdoors and getting back to the basics of living, without the temptation of trivial, time-wasting behaviours. I have had to learn to show acceptance of where I am in life and make the most out of it. I have also realised many of our habits come more from mind than matter. Issues that bothered me before, like the hair on my pillowcase, no longer exist! It has made me see things for what they really are, and how materialistic I was. I feel now that I have adjusted well to my situation, and that didn't happen overnight, but it has brought me back to my grass roots. Now I have a treasure box of amazing gems that I value greatly, and I'm sharing them with you.

Ya Gotta Laugh

Keeping up appearances

I don't know if you ever watched the English comedy television show *Keeping Up Appearances*? The show's main character is Hyacinth Bouquet (but we all know her name looks like 'Bucket'). She is always trying to keep up the façade of being of a higher social status than she really is, as a lot of people do in society. I suppose I am guilty of that. Not so much of putting across a higher status, but I do like to look nice. Along with keeping up with fashion to some degree, and a few blingy accessories, I like to put a little colour on my face. I personally think it shows that you have pride in yourself, and it makes you feel good at the same time.

I was never one for doing the whole kit and kaboodle, which can take some women an hour to do as they make themselves up. I mostly just applied eye liner, usually blue, and a smidge of mascara. Wipe on a bit of lippie and you're ready to go. I never blow dried my hair either; I am a wash and wear type of girl. Extremely low maintenance, I would say.

When I lost my sight, one of the grooming rituals that I liked to do was now a seemingly impossible task to perform. I mean, how could I ever apply eye liner and mascara when I couldn't see where I was putting it? At least my eyebrows weren't a concern. Well, they would have been if I didn't get them waxed, but my beautician prevents the infestation of large hairy caterpillars from growing on my face. Putting on makeup, though, was still a looming task for me.

I put my question to Vision Australia, and they soon set me up to learn how to put makeup on. I was still boggling as to how I would do this. Applying a brush to your eyelid is tricky at the best of times and now I was going to be doing it blindfolded, so to speak. I was certainly intrigued how this was going to pan out.

The foundation side of makeup was easy. A tinted moisturizer that comes in a measured pump action is perfect. The volume is measured with each squeeze so it's pretty hard to muck up. Plus, mine has an added sunscreen in it, so doubles up in action; not only making me look gorgeous with a smooth complexion, but also saving me from getting more wrinkles from sun damage. Now, you can't go past that, can you?

I will share with you the mysterious trade secret of how someone who can't see can create a majestic piece of artwork on the canvas of their face. 'Majestic' may be a little farfetched, but I still need my ego stroked at times, so I may as well do it myself. It's all done with the fingers. Yep, no need for any applicator brushes at all. Clever, huh? Use a different finger for each part of the eyelid, of course wiping off any eye shadow colour on your finger in between, or else you may end up looking like a clown! Always use a light patting motion over the area you need to cover. Never wipe, as this can make the application uneven. Simply by finger tapping over your lid, an amazingly even cover is reached. Feeling with one finger where the eyebrow is, you then place your highlighting shadow finger on the brow bone and pat away under there, following and feeling the hair line. Simple, right?

Mascara is easy too. Place the index finger of your other hand between your nose and eye. Then, with the mascara brush sticking on the finger so it doesn't move, you blink away, and mascara is applied on your lashes (and not all over your face).

It took some practicing to get the hang of it, but now I can put my makeup on in a car as we travel along, and it always turns out perfect. Well as far as I am concerned anyway! Besides, no one would be game enough to tell me otherwise, as they would be thinking, 'Poor woman, trying her best to look nice and she has made a complete botch of it!' At first, I used to try taking selfies of my eyes and sending them to my friend to ask if I had evenly applied my makeup, but taking the selfie in itself was a fiasco. I feel pretty confident I can do a good job on 'keeping up appearances,' anyway.

While on the topic of keeping up appearances, this is even more important now than ever before. You may be asking, why? Especially as I no longer work in the high school. Imagine for a moment what you would feel like if you were always being compared to a Miss World every time you went out? With

Miss World always looking beautiful, long bouncy locks of hair sweeping down over her perfect figure. No matter what she wore, she looked like a movie star queen. I think you would want to at least wear some eye-catching garments and perhaps a touch of makeup or at the least, a bit of lippie. I am sure you would want to try and hold some of your own ground in the looks stakes.

Having Rhian by myside is equivalent to having Miss World accompanying me at all times. We are told when training with them that the dog is meant to be invisible to other people. By that, I mean people are meant to completely ignore her and only talk to me. That's part of not distracting the working dog. Yep! that really works well. NOT. The truth of the matter is I become invisible, and everyone wants to talk to her. Loaded down with this heavy burden of having Miss World as my bestie and partner in life, I have the extra stress of having to look as glamorous as possible all the time. That is a tough and expensive image to maintain.

When Les queries why I needed to buy another outfit or some blingy jewellery, my simple answer is, I can't have Rhian getting all the attention and fuss all the time. I need to try and get noticed too. With this, he just shakes his head, as he knows how much fuss Rhian attracts. Man, I can tell you now it sure is tough trying to get some of that limelight on me!

Whenever I go anywhere with Rhian and a passer-by says, 'Oh, hello gorgeous,' obviously directing it to the dog, I quickly come back with, 'Oh, why thanks,' along with a chuckle. Then I often get hit back with a response like 'You look gorgeous too.' Yeah right, I know you only meant the dog, but I'll take whatever compliments I can get. You may laugh at this, but it can be quite hard on one's ego when your partner gets all the attention. That definitely calls for a beautiful new dress or shoes to be acquired. Wouldn't you agree? Keeping up appearances with a seeing eye dog is a tough gig but I guess somebody has to do it.

So if you come across a person with a seeing eye dog, please pay some attention to the invisible human before directing your focus to what you are really interested in, namely the dog. Just pretend, if you have to. It will still be received happily. A compliment about the person wouldn't go astray, either. It may very well be the saving grace for a person who may be feeling the need to go out and buy another outfit!

Colleen Ashby

Learning from my mistakes

Luckily for me, I am a quick learner. The saying that you learn best by the mistakes you make, I feel, is absolutely true. Since being blind, I can honestly say the mistakes I've made have been my greatest teachers. One might say I learned from the school of hard knocks. A few of those knocks were physical ones too, while others were things I just learned not to do any more.

As for the physical knocks, there were plenty of times I ended up with bruises on my left arm and (even more painful) my left leg. With no usable sight in my left eye, things like bus stops, bollards and signposts were the main fighting contestants in the ring. Jumping out from left field to do a surprise attack on me, they all thought they had me. My mind is sharp as a tack, however, and I am boasting here, so I learned my opponents' strategies. Like any good fight, I recorded these surprise encounters in my head, enabling me to swiftly dart away from any predictable left hooks coming my way.

We had a stack of palm tree stumps under our patio all huddled together, supposedly out of the way of any foot traffic. Like any team huddled together, however, these stumps secretly devised a game plan to defeat any attackers. They were especially strategic in their move to blindside me, pardon the pun! When I was playing with Rhian and running with her toy out onto our lawn, the stumps succeeded in tackling me to the ground. Running full boar into them, my left leg copped the brunt of this extremely painful tackle. I yelled out in excruciating pain then walked off the field, limping, with blood running down my leg. This later resulted in large black bruises. I had completely forgotten the stumps were there, and without seeing them on my left side, the offensive attack was a sneaky game play indeed.

I learned one lesson with a less harmful outcome when I was working at the school. I always had a sandwich bag of nuts in my drawer for snacks at morning tea. I had Rhian's dog kibble snacks in a bag as well. Returning from class for morning tea, I always gave Rhian a treat for her clever work. While I was getting my coffee mug prepared to make a cuppa, I too wanted a quick treat, as working with teenage children always made me ravenous. Picking up bag of nuts, I grabbed a handful and chucked them into my mouth. Two crunches and I immediately spat them into the bin, yelling in displeasure. Vicki came running in quickly to see what was wrong. I told her I just ate a mouthful of Rhian's dog kibble instead of my nuts! She only said if I had a fetish for eating dog kibble, I had better bring more along so Rhian didn't miss out!

You would think this would be lesson enough to be more careful about what I place in my mouth, but I guess sometimes my sharp-as-a-tack mind gets blunt. Only two days later, I repeated the exact same process. Even though I was careful to feel my nuts (lucky I'm not a bloke telling this story) before putting them in my mouth. Nope! Distastefully spitting them out once more, Vicki once again came in and told me if I really enjoyed eating dog kibble so much, I shouldn't hold back on this good stuff and should bring some out to share for morning tea!

The thing is that kibble and nuts are a similar shape. Along with being the same colour, well to me anyway! And as for smell, there really isn't much difference, either. I eventually learned my lesson and kept my nuts in the next drawer down, and I always made sure I had a good feel of my nuts before I ate them!

A slightly more expensive lesson was when I attempted cleaning out my bathroom cupboard myself. I was frustrated with not being able to find my items for personal beauty maintenance. I have mentioned before that I am extremely low maintenance in this area, but I still have a regime. Les had devised a strategy for me to be able to find my things. This was a large plastic container on top of the vanity bench. Like all plastic containers, soon everything ended up getting thrown in there and it turned into chaos.

Fumbling around all these jars of similar size and not knowing what they were, I made the executive decision to clean it out myself.

I opened a brown jar and smelled it. My olfactory senses were not registering any memory of this unpleasant odour. Presuming that my organic and natural face cream had gone off, I threw it in the bin. I came across another brown jar, and the fragrance of this one was extremely pleasurable to my olfactory senses. Yes, I will keep this creamy gem.

One week later, after having some acupuncture, the therapist told me to put some of the arnica and comfrey cream on my arm. I looked for my little brown jar of arnica, which I knew I had at home, as I had only bought it several weeks prior. Getting flustered as I rummaged through all my jars and bottles in my container on the bathroom bench, I yelled out to Les if he could come in and find it for me.

As Les was searching and reading all the labels out, I kept telling him I knew it was there somewhere. I only bought it a few weeks ago! Les confirmed it was not there, then walked out defeated by my antagonistic exasperation with not finding my jar.

Then a great bolt of lightning struck me and turned on that stupid lightbulb that reminded me of the little brown jar that I had thrown in the bin last week. Walking out to Les like a wimpy dog with its tail between its legs and head hung low, I apologised and told him how I had cleaned out the plastic container by myself and had thrown out the brown jar that I thought smelled like off face cream.

Not only did I have to go and buy another expensive jar of arnica, but also I had to eat humble pie for accusing Les of not being able to find something that I thought was there. The lesson learned here was not to clean out things without the guidance of a sighted person!

Ya Gotta Laugh

Leaving a voice message

Thank heaven for the amazing gift of the telephone. Now we can communicate with one another from anywhere in the world. When I was a child, the phone had the ten finger holes around the circular disk that you had to pull around to dial up the number you wanted. Then you would wait for the *brrr* sound as it rewound back to its starting position. I have fond memories of using one of those. Then came the push-button phone. Man, you felt pretty cool having a quick push-button in place of the old dial ones. Even better if you had one with a really long curly phone cord that enabled you to walk up to three metres away from the base. I never had one of those but loved seeing them in other people's houses. Let's skip forward twenty years and look at society now. Mobile phones you can carry anywhere with you at all times and just about do anything on them for any social engagement or entertainment. Now, where was I going with this chapter? Ah yes, that's right. Leaving a voice mail message.

When you need to use the Voice Over accessibility function on a phone, there are a number of gestures or hand actions to make it work. Putting this aspect aside, you also need to learn how to voice what you're announcing to Siri to make your message understandable.

The most important thing to make your message comprehensible is to punctuate it. Sounds silly, but if you simply voice your message with no punctuation, I can guarantee even you will have a tough time reading it. How you do this with Voice Over is quite simply to voice the punctuation. Let me give you an example: 'How are you doing today, question mark, I have been very well, coma, thank you, full stop, I can't believe the weather, exclamation mark.' It most probably seems absurd to you, but after a while you become extremely proficient at doing this. Like all repeated actions, it becomes second nature.

As I am so used to talking this way into my phone now, I need to be aware when to switch my punctuation cap off and on in my head. I will quite often make a phone call and need to leave a voice message. Having left my punctuation cap on, my message will go something like this: 'Hello, coma, this is Colleen Ashby, full stop, I was wondering if I could make an appointment, question mark.' Realising that I am talking and not texting, I will bumble my way through finishing my voice message. 'Sorry, comma, no, I didn't mean to punctuate this message. Just call me back, full stop. Sorry, it's just habit, full stop, bye.' I have even talked to people like this at times and was not even aware of what I was doing! This would have to be one of the downfalls of using Voice Over, but it is quite entertaining for listeners, most probably thinking I am playing a prank on them.

There is also a flipside to voice messages, and that is when I receive one. Often people will leave a message containing a number to call them back on. Basic formality, right? Let's take a look at how this works when you can only rely on your ears to get information.

One, I can't write the number down. Well, I can but I can't re-read what I have written. Two, I will often try and replay the message over and over to lock it into my memory bank, but if it is a long message, there is too much other information for me to decipher. The few times there has been a short, succinct message, I can replay it over several times and say the numbers in my head. However, when I then go to make the call, which includes Siri gabbing away at me to get this far, it's usually a case of 'Elvis has left the building,' and an incorrect number has been dialled. By this stage, I am generally in a worked-up state, especially if it was an important call to make. Teary with frustration, I have to just let it go, forget about it and wait until someone comes home to read the number out for me. By then, the company is usually closed for the day! Now, I bet you never thought about that aspect, did you?

Colleen Ashby

Mystifying the children

Working in the high school, one of my jobs was to walk around the children sitting at their desks and ask if they needed any help. This was easy, as they would just read the question and tell me what they didn't understand. Most of the children actually enjoyed asking me for help and were always polite and engaging. However, like most kids, some always wanted to try and cheat the system. One of the strict policies was no mobile phone use during class. Well, we all know how addicted people are to checking their phones every five seconds to see if there is a notification that may make them feel important or boost their ego, or to keep up with whatever the latest sensation is in the popular circle. They all think they have a secretive, stealthy way of checking their phone without being noticed, but they all assume wrong.

One of my greatest personal joys since losing my sight was to mystify the children! Remember, I still have a tiny bit of vision on my right side, not clear but enough to see shapes and colours. Therefore, I notice when a kid has their head tilted down towards their lap. Now there is no reason to tilt one's head unless you are wanting to look at something down there. Not having to be a Sherlock Holmes in this department, I would sneak up on their left, bend down and very quietly tell them to put it away unless they wanted to have it confiscated. Standing back up, I could see them looking up at me while my side was facing them. Obviously totally bewildered as to how I could see they were on their phones, I reiterated to put it away. The next best part for me, to complete my great satisfaction of mystifying them, was when they would then turn their heads around to their mates and shrug their shoulders. Bamboozled as to how I knew they were on their phones when I couldn't see. It always left me killing myself laughing on the inside. They never knew about my five per cent vision in my right eye.

Keeping up the mystifying charade, when some of them would ask how I knew they were on their phone, my response was that I may not be able to see but my hearing was super sensitive as a result, and I could hear their fingers tapping on the phone screen! This mystified them even further.

You have to be able to have a bit of fun and be an enigma when you lose one of your senses. That is what can make it all worthwhile.

Another particularly satisfying account with some of the children was when I was in the classroom with Rhian. To set the scene for you, dear reader, I must inform you Rhian had done twelve months in customs puppy training before being transferred over to SED to do another twelve months in their puppy training. I like to boast she has a double degree! Back in the classroom, there are always a few kids who like to think they are cool with talking about drugs. Boasting how much they smoked pulling bongs on the weekend or how much dope they have, you know the ones. They are in every class or group you meet.

As I walked past a group of kids (usually the raggedy, tough crowd, fond of crude language and always full of bravado), I would pause at one of their desks for a moment. I would bend down and announce, loud enough so all their mates could hear, that they had better not have any drugs in their bag. Looking up at me, they would give some smart alec response, like so what if they did? I would assertively state that Rhian was originally a customs dog and could sniff out any drugs on them or in their bag.

Sudden gasps of surprise, they were now fearing they may get caught out by the dog. The word quickly got around to all of the larrikin crowd that Rhian was a drug-sniffing dog and they had better be careful. Man, I loved performing that little sketch, it always brought me immense pleasure. I knew full well she hadn't been professionally trained in that department, but I wasn't giving that away!

Ya Gotta Laugh

No rissoles

I was feeling stupendously excited, as I had just received my first three hundred printed books of *I Can See Clearly Now*. My book launch was in three days and now I had the exciting and official task of signing the books. It still didn't feel real that I had accomplished writing my own memoir. I mean, really, how many people can say they have written and published a book? I had done it in a matter of months, and now was in the final stage of being an author and signing my name.

The suggestion was made that I pre-sign a number of books, I thought it was a clever idea, so if people wanted personal inscriptions, it would leave me more time to do this. You may be thinking, how do I write and sign a book. The answer is simple. I have been writing my whole life. Just because I have lost my vision, doesn't mean I have lost the art of writing.

There are a few adjustments or criteria for me being able to write, though. The main item on the list is silence. The reason for this is once again quite simple. Once my pen is on the paper, I need to rehearse in my head what I want to write. Then, with words in a sequence, I can start putting pen to paper. Naturally, spelling each letter out as I write in my head, I know where I am up to. If the silence is broken or my thoughts are interrupted, then it all goes out the window. I can't read what I have just written, nor do I remember where I am up to writing the word. So long as my pen never leaves the paper, I am alright. So, here I was signing, 'No regrets, C Ashby.' I had already done two hundred books. I was sitting at the kitchen bench with Les and Scott, who were discussing cooking dinner. The conversation revolved around making rissoles. As their bantering got louder, and the word rissoles kept coming to the forefront, my brain couldn't maintain its concentration of 'No regrets.' Yep, I signed the book, 'No rissoles, C Ashby!'

Realising what I had just done, I told the cooks to shut up and get on quietly with cooking the bloody rissoles and not to say that word again!

All the books were successfully signed, except one. At the book launch I did a Question and Answer with the publisher, then I was allowed to take the floor for a bit of a laugh. With this, I relayed the story above. I stated that some lucky person would behold an exceptionally special signature on their book, which may be worth a lot of money one day. A bit of boasting, my plumage feathers were getting fluffed up here. I had to cover my tracks somehow.

Well, at the signing table, the chattering excitement was about who had the book with 'No rissoles' in it. A bit like winning the golden ticket in a Willy Wonka chocolate bar. I even had one person, when I asked what they wanted me to inscribe to them, reply that 'No rissoles' would be fantastic!

I have signed other books at different events and when it comes time to inscribing messages, I may come across as a sergeant major barking orders. Naturally, they are interested in talking to me, but I state, 'Now, you have to be quiet while I sign your book, otherwise I don't know where I am up to in writing and can't see to continue.' With this, they stand silently until I have finished signing the book. I am sure they understand and are most probably amazed how I even do that!

Speaking of signing my signature when I have to sign documents, I just tell the person to put my pen and hand on the place to sign, and away I go. I laugh and say things like, 'So I just signed my house mortgage over to you,' or 'I've just signed my offshore account to you.' This generally lightens the mood. However, one day I was in a surgeon's room signing a consent paper and he asked what do I do about signing? I simply told him to place my pen and hand where X marks the spot and we're good to go. He discerningly sat back and told me that he didn't think that was legal. I reassured him I did it all the time. I have even signed my bank accounts and mortgage over to people. He still didn't seem to take this lightly and after I signed the papers, he told me he wrote that the person signing was blind. He wanted to cover his tracks safely.

I'm not sure if it is legal or not, but I am quite happy to sign my name when needed. So far, I haven't lost any money from my secret offshore account in the Bahamas, yet!

Ya Gotta Laugh

Once you go black, you never go back

When you first lose sight, the usual mobility aid is a long cane. This is always the fallback plan for getting around. I didn't want a standard white cane so opted for a very out-there, bright, hot pink cane with a purple ball. I wasn't going to be defined as a typical blind person. No way, baby! This mobility aid is a great item indeed, as it tells you when the land's layout changes and there are slopes, bumps or obstacles in your way. It does have its limitations, though, as a directional guiding tool. You still need someone with you to give you directions, but it remains a fantastic apparatus to have all the same.

When the opportunity of getting a seeing eye dog arose, I was full of apprehension. Dog hair was one of my main concerns, along with how much hassle and work would having this dog be? Would I use it enough to warrant the responsibility?

And how will my pet dog get on with me taking the new dog out all the time? It certainly wasn't an easy decision to make and even when I was flying to Melbourne, I still wasn't sure I had made the right decision.

Let's fast-forward a year. By now, I had flown to Queensland twice with Rhian on holidays, and then to Sydney for all the touristy things over there too. I was working in the high school with her, and she was my companion whilst walking to work in the mornings. Rhian and I are so in sync with one another that I hardly even have to tell her too many commands. She just knows what to do.

The advantage of a seeing eye dog over a cane is that she can weave you in and out of obstacles smoothly and find things like escalators and lifts. She remembers where I like to go, and it is just like having my bestie with me all the time. Two girls having an outing together.

I thought having a cane rolling from side to side made people get out of the way. Having a dog is like Moses parting the Red Sea water. Everyone stops and looks or quickly jumps out of the way as we confidently stroll through shopping centres and busy places. I tell anyone with me to just follow in my wake as Rhian boldly paves the way. I would compare having a cane to seeing a local homegrown circus; still entertaining and enjoyable. Having a dog, though, is like going to see *Cirque du Soleil*, with all the awe and wonder about it.

There have been two times when I couldn't use Rhian. Each episode was for a couple months each. One time she had broken her toe and was in a cast for eight weeks, and the more recent was when I had shoulder surgery and was out of action for three months. On both these occasions I had to revert to my trusty hot pink cane, and man, it was like going back to the Dark Ages. With Rhian, I can walk freely, chat to whoever is with me and not worry about hitting things. I tried doing the same with the cane and ended up running into sandwich boards and tripping over. I would head off in the wrong direction, my friend having to direct me back, and my confidence quickly diminished when I was out in busy areas. It was not only the issue of getting around independently that bothered me. I didn't like leaving my bestie at home by herself when I knew she would be fretting for me. I think it is worse than leaving a child to be babysat.

Now that you have a comparison of the two major mobility aids, you can obviously see that once you go black, you never go back! Just a sidenote for anyone with a seeing eye dog of another colour, the same rule still applies. I just think this particular saying fits my story perfectly.

Colleen Ashby

Playing battleships at dinner time

Eating a meal is something we all do without even thinking about it. Our parents taught us how to feed ourselves at an early age and most importantly how to perform the task making as little mess as possible. Dining etiquette is high up there on the list of society's social standards. What I have come to realise is how much our eyesight plays a part in that role. 'You eat with your eyes' is a longstanding phrase that goes further than what you think.

We use our eyes to savour the scrumptious meal before us, taking in the tantalising colours, shapes and arrangement. Smell also plays a huge role, but I have come to understand that we mostly eat with our eyes. Now, let's put the aesthetics factor heightening the enjoyment of the meal aside, and consider how we use our eyes for strategic purposes. That is, of course, to tell us where the food is and what we are about to eat.

There were many times when I first lost vision and was still in hospital that I had to ask the nurse what was on the plate that I was about to eat. This is one visual component. The other aspect is working out where the different foods are on the plate. We all have our own quirky little habits of how we like to eat our food. We tend to save our favourite part for last, don't we? To do that, you need to know where it is on the plate. Hmmm! I bet you never thought about that, did you?

One of the most frustrating times for me is at Christmas or buffet-style meals. Asking the person with me to put the several types of food on my plate is one thing. The next is sitting down and not being able to work out what the different foods are. When I come across one that I decide to save for last, as it is highly scrumptious, I cunningly move the plate around so I can come back to it later. Unfortunately, when you have a crowded plate it inevitably finds its way stealthily into other food on the plate, never to be tasted separately again.

A clock-style system is used to tell a vision-impaired person where the various food items are. Meat would be at, say, twelve o'clock, peas at three, carrots at six and potato nine. This at least gives the person some idea where to find the various bits of food. That's fine, but the other issue is when you have small items such as corn, peas or any other diced-up vegetable. These are not only tricky to load onto your fork (hopefully they will reach your mouth without all falling off), but even harder to stab with a fork. I am usually the last to finish my meal, as it takes longer for me to load up and balance the fork only to then have it fall off as I endeavour to place it all in my mouth.

Another aspect amusing for the family but frustrating for me is trying to stab vegetables with my fork. After eating part of my meal, I was wanting to eat my carrots. As I stabbed around on my plate, Scott would say, 'Nearly, no, to the right. Up a little bit. No, over to the left now.' I was now getting a wee bit frustrated, wanting to get on with eating my dinner, so I snapped back at Scott, 'Just bloody load my fork up with some carrots!' As I handed my fork over to him, he jovially announced, 'You wouldn't be much good at playing battleships, Mum. I have never seen someone stab all around their plate and still miss the food!' We all just had to sit and have a good laugh about it.

Ya Gotta Laugh

Politically incorrect, but totally funny

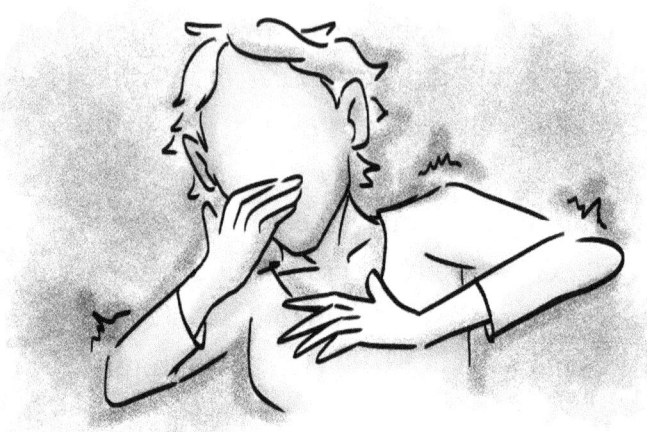

When I was working in the high school, we had a new relief deputy come in for a semester. Walking through the front office with Rhian by my side as I usually did each morning, one of the staff introduced me to the new deputy. She was standing in the hallway, so I stopped to say hello. To my utmost surprise she was very vibrant and extremely jovial. As we were both boisterously bouncing off introductions to one another and already relaxed in easy communication, it felt as if we had known each other for a long time.

After a few minutes of exchanged laughter and banter, she let me know (in a manner that was very unobtrusive) that something was happening that was most probably not socially acceptable behaviour. 'Colleen, your dog has been sniffing my crotch!' This embarrassing situation had happened on more than one occasion before then. I quickly did a mental scan as to how best to make light of the awkwardness.

Within what seemed like minutes but was only nanoseconds, I retorted back, 'Well, what have you got packed up there? She did twelve months in Customs puppy training.' Knowing that this was a totally crude and politically incorrect thing to say, I had obviously really stretched the limits to how a staff member converses with a person in a superior position. I waited in bated breath for her response. After a short pause, as her brain had obviously just scrambled through what I put to her, the response was a huge rapture of belly laughter! I smiled with great relief and quietly giggled.

She chortled, 'Oh Colleen, you have to work that little number. That is so funny!' Now knowing she had a wicked sense of humour, I proceeded down the hallway, listening to her laughing and telling other staff members an account of what had just been exchanged. I had a smile on my face, glad it all ended well. I know that what I said was not appropriate and some people would have taken great offense, but sometimes you just must take a chance, roll the dice and hope it is a winner.

A previous incident similar to that one, occurred when I was returning home from Melbourne. I had been there meeting (and learning how to handle) my new partner in crime, Rhian. I was new to the behaviours and how to handle her. Like any relationship, it takes time to develop that innate deep connection, when you just know the other better than yourself.

So I had my trainer with me at the airport, along with Rhian by my side. As we waited at the airport gates, ready to board the flight, the boarding attendant came over to check if there was anything we needed before boarding. He stood in front of the two of us, conversed for a few minutes, then turned and went to get things sorted.

After he left, the trainer leaned over and quietly whispered in my ear, 'Colleen, that attendant was very professional and polite. Rhian had her nose in his crotch the whole time and he never lost eye contact with either you or me.' With a quiet giggle, both of us laughing hysterically on the inside, I also had a slight glow of embarrassment. I felt awkward about the situation but as I couldn't see that she was doing it, I guess I have a disclaimer about her behaviour. We boarded and had an exceptionally smooth flight home.

I would just like to add that we have done further training regarding this issue and can now meet people without Rhian behaving inappropriately. Anyway, in the big scheme of things, for all the amazing things she does for me, I think a bit of occasional crotch sniffing is not too bad a price to pay.

Colleen Ashby

Power points and candles

How we all take for granted the amazing technology of electricity and its many functional uses. Just plug the power cord into the socket and presto! Nearly any desire you have, to create something or get a job done, electricity can make it happen. In fact, without electricity we would have a very hard time trying to function in modern times. Everything comes to a standstill when the power goes out. It's like our modern existence is nearly totally reliant upon the powerful god of electricity, who may giveth lovingly but then also taketh away when angry, shutting off from us. We are all at the mercy of electricity.

You would think just simply putting a plug into the socket is an uncomplicated and basic task, wouldn't you? Think again. Give it a go with your eyes shut. Not so easy. In fact, power points are one of my pet hates. You have to feel the prongs of the plug, find the flat straight bottom prong and then, with your other hand, feel around to line it up with the matching slot in the power point. The fact that two hands are required to accomplish this awkward matching process, while you are leaning stretched over a bench, makes it all the more difficult. Note to the reader: Before trying this at home, make sure you have the power point switched off. Les is always telling me off for sticking my fingers all around and in the power point socket! I haven't got electrocuted yet, though, I may add.

The other tricky part can be the position of the power point. Up high on benchtop level is somewhat easier, very slightly though, compared to fossicking around lower, near the floor. Those ones are nearly impossible to do without getting into some raging state where you get possessed by a demonic entity that has you speaking in tongues, or very politically incorrect and frowned-upon language. My dog soon exits the building, fearing she may get some of this demonic wrath directed her way! I promise you I never get frustrated with her, and I call her back to give her a great big cuddle, or peanut butter on her bone as a special treat. This makes her forget all about that demonic episode quickly.

Now you have some idea about what it's like trying to match two things together, like toothpaste on toothbrushes or power points in plugs, well, now comes another one. Try lighting a candle or the end of an incense stick! Yep, you guessed it; not so easy. Lighting the match is simple, no brainer there at all. Lining the flame up with the wick, especially if it's a big candle in a glass holder, you've got Buckley's of matching that little pair up first time. If I'm lucky, I may light it with the second match, and I use the long ones too. Incense sticks are equivalent in the amount of frustration felt. On a scale of one to five, one being easy and five expressing extreme explosive outbursts of frustration, I would score it a four.

Once you have the candle lit, even trying to blow the match out is another task in itself. Ridiculous, I know, but it's true. I'm not making this up. Again, if you don't believe me, blindfold yourself and give it a go. I have burned my fingers or dropped the match on several occasions due to not being able to blow the damn thing out in time!

I may not always have much success at lighting the wick of the candle, but the task certainly knows how to light my fuse and blow me up in no time at all!

Ya Gotta Laugh

Raise your hand if you have a question

When I returned to work after having the transplant and losing my vision, the school thought it would be a great idea for me to introduce myself to the new year 7's entering the school. Not only for them to get to know me, but also for them to be able to ask any questions about either a heart transplant or life with no vision. I agreed it was an ingenious idea to help alleviate any curiosity or beliefs they may have of either issue.

This teaching intervention took place in a DigiTech class, where students learn digital technologies. One of the devices the students use is the iPad. I suggested to the teacher that after my talk and questions from the students, I could show them how to activate the Voice Over utility and we could all practice how to use Siri to do things. Fun and interactive, this would work well.

Entering the classroom with my bright pink cane, I was led to the front of the room to be introduced. I folded up my cane, so the students could also see how neatly it folded up, and placed it on the table. I told them briefly of my background, which included the heart transplant surgery and becoming legally blind due to complications during this process. I then asked the class if they had any questions about any part of my story. I mean, how many people have come across someone who has either had a heart transplant or lost their vision? I know I certainly hadn't before it happened to me. I wanted to be as open and honest with any enquiries they may have had.

I said to the class if they had any questions to just raise their hand. After waiting for what seemed like several minutes with no response, I was beginning to wonder if they really had no interest in the matter. A glum feeling of disappointment came over me. I felt like a failure despite trying to engage with the children. All I could do was stand there and look out at the dark gloomy void of nothingness before me. Then the teacher announced, 'Mrs Ashby, we have quite a few hands up to answer.'

Of course, it was not that the students weren't interested, I simply forgot about the issue of having no sight! I couldn't see their raised hands. I couldn't see anything at all! It sounds ridiculous, but I forgot I couldn't see. It's sounding weird, right? But you just tend to continue doing what you did before and wonder why it's not working.

Relieved with this welcome lightbulb moment, my brain switched to problem-solving mode. Jokingly, I said to the class, 'Of course, I can't see your hands up, so the teacher will have

Ya Gotta Laugh

to choose for me. Then you can ask your question.' The teacher announced the student's name and before I knew it, questions were rolling in. Good ones too, filled with genuine queries.

After concluding an extremely noisy session of playing on the iPad using Voice Over, the children in raptures of laughter when Siri announced what the emoji icons were, I was beaming inside with pride. The children were engaged and had their curiosity satisfied. I also felt that the students would now feel confident enough to converse with me if they chanced across me either within the school or out in the community.

I've had to become quite inventive with resolving problematic situations. Some of those occasions were when I decided to join a public speaking group in my local community. One of the tasks was to choose a person, wearing a name tag, and put a proposition to them. Obviously, I can't read the name tags or even point to someone sitting in the group. This is where I had to put my thinking cap on and produce a clever solution.

My first moment of creativity was to use playing cards. I got Les to pull out the top five ranking cards. Ten, Jack, Queen, King and Ace. I only had to ask five people and I could easily remember these cards. To make it more intriguing, I handed a card to each person and told them not to show anyone else and place it flat down on the table in front of them. When it was my turn to take the floor, I proposed a question and then announced the playing card that was going to have to answer it. There was soon a bustle of activity as each person flipped their card and then checked with the neighbouring person to see if they were the lucky winner. I would equate it to playing bingo and having to call out winner! At the end of the session the accumulative feedback was that it was more exciting and a refreshing concept for a change. Everyone experienced a genuine sense of enjoyment with this activity.

At another meeting, I wanted to change it up, to keep it interesting. I decided to get some coloured fuzzy pipe cleaners. I got Les to choose five assorted colours and tell me what they were. I used the same concept of getting people to hide their pipe cleaner so no one else could see it. This too created a lot of excitement and anticipation as people checked their own colour, then looked around at others to see if they had the lucky one.

This inventive brainstorming actually resulted in a far more fun and interactional meeting which would never have occurred otherwise. Losing my sight has really been a gift that keeps giving great little gems to me.

Ya Gotta Laugh

Rockabilly rebel

Music and dancing have been a golden thread throughout my life, playing guitar and then keyboard, or organ, as we had back in the seventies and eighties. I've been ballroom dancing in and out through the years, along with rockabilly and rock and roll jive. I ran a clogging group, which is like tap dancing, and then became a fitness instructor teaching aerobics followed by Zumba. I have always had music and dance in the forefront of my being. I honestly think I would die if there weren't music for me to listen to everyday. The magic of the tone and rhythm has limitless influence over anyone in its reach. It can lift you up when you're feeling down, or it can make you feel sad even when you're not. It can calm you down or rev you up. It has always been my magic bullet, keeping me on track in my emotional wellbeing.

This magical golden thread was my lifeline, especially in the first year after losing sight. When those long, lonely days rolled by one after another and I had little capability for doing simple things for myself, I drew on this thread. Listening to the radio (or if I managed to put a play list on), I would live in my mind. Hearing the songs that took me back to the ballroom dance floor, I would dance with my partner rhythmically and be consumed by the music. I could dance in my head for hours and be in that euphoric state of previous years. At times I would even physically get up and waltz or cha-cha around the kitchen and dining room area. It was the only way I knew of staying on top of my emotional state.

I was a quick and natural visual learner. I was fluid at picking up choreography. Natural rhythm flows through every cell in my body. With this in mind once I lost sight, I never lost this magic tempo within me. It wasn't long before my yearning to do the light fandango was nagging me all the time. It was my link back to what I loved before, and I needed to revitalise this passion. My first rendezvous was with rock and roll jive.

A friend had been going at beginner level, and I was happy with that, as at least I would be dancing again. I told her I didn't want to use my cane. I was worried if people saw I was blind, I may be treated differently or not get a dance. With that in mind, together we walked in and paid our dues, then proceeded to buy a drink at the bar and mingle in with all the other dancers.

Ya Gotta Laugh

Time to hit the ballroom blitz. Well, not quite, but you get what I mean. After the initial line up of men on one side and women on the other, we watched the instructors display the moves we would be learning, and the basics began. Watching out of the corner of my right eye, I was able to get the context of what we were learning. I already knew how to do this from my years of dancing and teaching ballroom. I was revved and ready to show off my fancy footwork. I paired up with a male walking across the dance floor and was soon jiving away merrily, singing to the song and just enjoying being back in the rhythm of life.

It wasn't long before some of the more experienced male dancers commented on how well I danced. This of course just went straight to my head, and I felt like the dancing queen being sought after by the men! Yeah baby, I was back in the game. Move over, Ginger Rogers! On some of the weeks when there were more women than men, I made my big reveal. Tired of waiting for a dance through the rotations, I stood with my back to the middle and grabbed the next female to come along. Though she was obviously unsure of me as I held out my hand to bring her into position, I reassured that I was doing the male's part.

Rhythm running like electricity through my veins, my body was ready to launch my partner into the best groove she ever had. So I wouldn't launch her into oncoming dancing rockets, which did occur several times, I moved out into the centre. Never too much collateral damage occurred, and my secret remained safe. All the women I danced with were surprised how well I led, and I had better rhythm than most of the men. Once the beat pulses through my being, anyone in my field is in for a fantastic time!

Not big-noting myself here, but I am a damn good dancer, even if I do say so myself!

I got away without anyone finding out that I couldn't see. That was easy as when you dance you don't really make eye contact all the time as you're weaving in and out of moves. No one ever expected it. There were two men that were impressed with my fluidity and grace. I decided to tell them and that was a shock for them, but they still loved dancing with me.

I soon got bored with this dancing, though, as I really wanted to go up a level and get into trickier moves, but the friend I went with wanted to stay in the beginners. When you know your own capability and are kept down at a lower level, it quickly becomes boring. Time to find a new challenge.

My friend Deb found a class of West Coast Swing starting up in Kalamunda. Deciding to give this brand new genre of dancing a go, off we went together to check it out.

It had a completely different beat to what I had ever danced to before, along with a unique style in counting and grip. It was a challenge for me, which I loved. Creeping up the ranks quickly, I was moving into difficult moves. One of the instructors gave me a pointer when I was dancing with him. He told me that when he held his right hand out, it was a signal to place my left hand in his. My flat response was that I would, but I couldn't see his hand. I was legally blind. Well, you should have seen his response as he fumbled around trying to work out how he was going to give me signals for the moves. It really flabbergasted him but at the same time amazed him that I could dance so well with this limitation.

Ya Gotta Laugh

I do love getting a kick out of people when I tell them this little secret of mine. Both astonishment and curiosity ramble around in their mind as to how I can be doing things. Another reason I don't always like informing people about my sight is because when they find out most of them do feel more hesitant when they interact with me. Better off not knowing, I feel, is the best remedy, at least until they really get to know me well.

There was another dance encounter that occurred early on after losing my sight. I was in Perth City at the Summer night food markets. With my guiding hot pink cane and my girlfriend by my side, we ventured into the delightful vibe of this festive event. Surrounded by the aromas of the sweet and spicy blends of foods, the bustling people chatting and enjoying one another's company, along with the sounds of different music and rhythms. It was a warm sultry evening and I immersed myself into every sensory stimulation I could conceive. Then I heard the magic mambo rhythm echoing across the crowd. Asking my friend to find where it was coming from, we made our way to this live Latin band.

Not being able to hold in the magic beat any longer, I told my friend I wanted to dance and asked if there were any other people dancing. She replied there was only a female band member doing Latin style moves, dressed up in a casual Caribbean outfit, with the band all wearing bright floral shirts behind her. Unable to hold the electric pulses that came from this energetic beat, I had to do it.

Folding up my cane, I handed it over to my friend and began dancing in the vacant floor space. Singing along to *Mambo No. 5*, muscle memory kicked in and I was doing Salsa footwork. I was in my own world with my hips swaying, feet moving, singing. Euphoria rose inside of me. It was so easy to be in my own world because with no vision, I couldn't see the crowd of people looking on. I only knocked the bucket that held money the audience donated twice. Luckily, the bucket never tipped over and spilled money everywhere. I was then aware of it and kept myself further forward. The female dancer came over to dance closer to me and seemed to be pleased that someone was up joining in.

As the song came to an end, buzzing with energy, I grabbed my cane from my friend, unfolded it and began walking away with her. She told me the expression on people's faces watching me as I walked away with a blind cane was priceless. She felt self-conscious for me but was in awe that I was game enough to get up there and dance in front of everybody. I simply replied that it was easy when you couldn't see any of them! A great benefit, or hidden gem, indeed.

Another funny little encounter I had early on after losing sight was when a girlfriend and I decided to hit the dance floor together. I had been wanting to listen to some music and dance, no matter what the situation or style. Free dancing or simply bopping around was good enough for me, I just had to get some rhythm through me and move with it.

Eventually we came across a small bar with a live guitar player singing and playing some pretty cool riffs and rhythms. We went inside and found a small dance floor with a few large wine barrels in each corner. A drink to get into the mood was the magic potion chosen. I personally needed nothing to get me up dancing, but my friend was a wee bit apprehensive about hitting the dance floor. So, to keep her company until she was ready to go, I had a drink too.

Let's just say that it took quite a few drinks to get her loose enough to let the tempo take over her. Finally getting into the groove, it was time for a music break. The obvious thing to do is down another drink. By now, I didn't care if she came up or not, I would just hit the floor myself. Swaying away, I noticed that a male had come into my personal body space and was strutting his swanky moves around me, like a peacock dancing, showing off his flamboyant tail feathers. I continued to dance by myself until he took my hand and began to properly dance with me, jiving and turning me. I was loving it.

My only regret was that I had one or two too many drinks than I should have, to be able to keep my balance, especially with the twirling circular moves. When he spun me out, I spun too quickly and tumbled into the large wooden wine barrel. Quickly recomposing myself, I was back in his dance grip once more. To show him my full talent, I did of course recreate this stunning barrel move one more time, just to show off my cool grooves. Laughing, with a few 'wahoos' and a smile as wide as the Cheshire Cat, he joined in and thought it great! I thought this would be the end of him wanting to dance with me when the next break came up.

He took me back to my seat with my girlfriend, then asked if I would dance with him when the music started again. Extremely surprised at this request, I answered of course I would.

My head was spinning and my girlfriend was in hysterics at my daring and outrageous dance moves. Both killing ourselves laughing, I told her to join me on the floor, but she told me that she was entertained enough watching my antics.

I did have another very cool set of dances with my newfound Fred Astaire, intoxicated or not, I loved every minute of it. Even inebriated, I was still a bloody fantastic dancer, and you don't need to ask anyone else who was there for their opinion either! Take my word for it.

When it was time to leave, my friend decided it may be a better idea if I didn't unfold my cane (which had been sneakily hidden in her bag) until I got out onto the street. It may have been a little embarrassing for the guy to learn he was dancing with a blind person! Now that, you have to laugh at!

Ya Gotta Laugh

Total devotion or separation anxiety?

Throughout history, dogs have represented true love, protection and loyalty. They have stood by man's side for centuries as true companions. They are also a reminder of playfulness through their interactions and ways of showing us the importance of enjoying life. Truly man's best friend. I know that every dog owner will state that their dog is the most loyal and loving dog ever, and I can't dispute that. Rhian, though, I feel, takes it to a whole new level.

Right from the get-go, I felt a deep connection with her. It really was as if we had lived previous lifetimes together and were once again reunited. We hit it off right from our very first encounter. Even the trainer told me that she had never seen a pair match up so quickly and easily before. Rhian and I were doing things together much quicker than the anticipated standard training time. We were back together strutting our stuff with ease and synchronicity. Besties side by side again as life would have it.

My first awareness of her strong connection with me was in the first four days. When you are learning how to handle your seeing eye dog, you can only take them out whilst with the trainer. You are allowed, however, to go for a walk around the area with your cane and tether your dog in the house. Needing to get some exercise, I would go for a walk around the block. As I would turn around the last corner about four houses from where I was staying, I could hear a dog howling at the top of its lungs. Who would let a dog carry on like that? I felt a slight rage at the cruelty of leaving a dog so distressed, howling like a wolf at the moon. When I opened my front door, Rhian's woeful howl echoed down the tall, long hallway.

Feeling bad finding her in such a distressed state, I went up to her quickly and got on the floor to cuddle and rub her ears as she lovingly licked my face in relief. The trainer told me to try a distraction before I next left for a walk, such as putting some peanut butter on her nylon bone. This may solve the problem as she would be able to focus on something she enjoyed and could destress by chewing the bone.

Well, sad to say, the bone was of no help at all and after two more tries leaving her for a walk, I would still come around the corner to hear the lone wolf miserably howling at the moon! I couldn't bear to do that anymore. It just wasn't fair on her.

Let's jump forward a few years and see if things have settled down somewhat? Much to my surprise, I think Rhian has reached an even higher state of devotion! I did think she would settle down somewhat, knowing the longer we have been together, the more secure she has felt. I was completely wrong in that assumption. Let me give you a few examples.

Whenever I need to have any medical procedures such as ultrasounds or heart echoes, Rhian is extremely curious and concerned with what the person is doing to me on the bed. She never settles and will keep checking on me and giving reassuring licks on my arm, as if to say, 'It's okay, I've got your back.' When I'm in the dentist's chair or getting podiatry check-ups, she will eyeball the stranger who is tampering with her guardian. Especially when those high-pitched drills or buffing tools start up, her unwavering eye contact with the perpetrator is unnerving. That is what they tell me during the session.

Her most recent and best performance expressing total devotion was when I needed to have a CT scan. I had previously done these, so Rhian knew what to expect. Entering the room with the scanner, I was shown to the bed that takes you into the tunnel. As I was lying down and getting into position, Rhian jumped up onto the bed as well. The technician found this entertaining, calling her off with a giggle. I told the technician to take her lead and she would go with her behind the safety office. This scan was a quick process of five minutes, if that. When the technician and Rhian re-entered the room, Rhian exuberantly jumped up on the side of the bed and lavished me in slapping licks all over my neck and face. The technician laughed over Rhian's reaction during this whole event. She said it was endearingly surprising to her that the whole time Rhian was out of sight from me, she never stopped whining. A superb performance of total devotion. I guess that five minutes is five minutes too long to be away from me!

You may be thinking these are all situations where strange and unfamiliar things are being done to me. Well, I will show you an example where she has a choice of having some much-loved and anticipated free time.

In the afternoons when Les returns from work, we have a routine. A cup of tea with a read of the newspaper is his time to unwind from the day's events. Rhian knows that he has the keys and free time is always associated with Les and the car. She will patiently wait on her bed until his cup of tea is finished, then she initiates her first tactical move.

The newspaper still up in reading position, she will sit directly in front of him and intently stare. Les hides behind the newspaper, knowing her game, and waits for the next move. Nudging his leg with her nose, she gives a low whine. He pops his head over and asks her what she wants. When he returns to reading his paper, Rhian brings out her big guns. A toy in her mouth makes for a great battering ram to bring down that newspaper. Whacking the paper with her toy, she moves from side to side in a determined way of getting Les's attention. Eventually, game won by Rhian, it's time for fun! Jasper will be barking and jumping in gleeful anticipation while Rhian paces excitedly, waiting for shoes to go on feet, and there is movement at the station!

Now, if Les goes out to the car before I am ready, will Rhian get into the car for her much-wanted and loved part of her day? You guessed it. Nope! Les can be calling her, Jasper already in the car, but she will be torn between staying with me or having the time of her life. She frantically runs back inside to find where I am and whines at me as if to say, 'Hurry up or we will miss out!' It seems I still win over fun free time. Luckily for her, she has never missed out on enjoying her free time.

I have tossed up over the past four years since being matched with Rhian if it is more a case of separation anxiety or true devotion. Most probably a bit of both. Whatever the case, I can't bring myself to leave her, knowing how dependant she is on me for her own mental wellbeing. I guess this is a win-win situation for both of us. I love her with every ounce of my body, as I know she does me. I am calling it total devotion on both our parts. Not man's best friend, but mine!

Colleen Ashby

Now just look at the camera

I am not too sure that I would ever make it on the cover of *Rolling Stone* magazine, though Dr Hook went on about trying to get on it. Not because I'm not famous enough (well, we both know that I'm definitely not, but that is not the point here!), but for the simple fact that the camera man would be pulling his hair out trying to work with me.

I had never even contemplated that I wasn't looking at the camera. I could see, well, to some degree, the person taking the photo out of the corner of my right eye. Of course, I was looking at the camera as far as I was concerned! Initially, I never knew how far to the right I was actually turning my head, but even once I was made aware of this, I still couldn't work out where the camera was to look at it.

Ya Gotta Laugh

The first professional encounter I had was when I was going on a television show and they wanted to take some photos for public media.

Standing there, all glammed up with gorgeous clothes on, hair and makeup professionally done, I was feeling like a glamour girl, to be idolised by many. There I was, trying different poses with my trendy hot pink cane. Just like the super models do with a prop to play with, I posed and smiled like the Cheshire Cat. Man, I was feeling on top of the world, thinking I was doing a fantastic job. Then I heard the camera man, somewhere in the distance say, 'Now, just look at the camera.'

What do you mean, look at the camera? I am already doing that, you idiot, I thought in my head. 'Where is the camera?' I asked. Obviously just comprehending that I was blind, he had one of those aha moments, realising he had to direct my head position.

'Look straight ahead,' he said, adjusting my position slightly as I glared into the grey blank space that was before me. 'Now, a little more to the left,' was the direction. As I moved my head, I heard, 'No, the other way. Good, back a little. Great, hold it there!' He sounded exasperated. I was now seeing the comedic scenario that had been evolving and began to laugh. Thankfully, so did the camera man. He had never had to deal with this issue before.

When I am in a selfie with friends, it's easier to get my eyes pretty close to looking straight at the camera. The close distance makes it have a better success rate. I always tend to have a great big grin from ear to ear. I do this hoping that people will be directed at my gorgeous smile and not notice where my eyes are looking.

Only recently I had to have another professional photoshoot at home. The photographer knew I was blind, so was semi-prepared for what he was in for. As he set up his equipment, I waited all glammed up again for my exciting photoshoot. He took a few practice shots for lighting adjustment and realised I wasn't looking into the camera. He had planned a trick to remedy this issue, however, and pulled it out of his hat, so to speak.

The photographer, sounding chuffed that he had thought of such an ingenious idea, revealed his magic trick. 'I brought a bright torch along, so you have a bright light to find and focus on. Okay, can you see the light?' he excitedly asked.

Looking directly in that vast, grey blank space, my answer was 'No.' Disappointed that his magic trick failed, he put his torch away and had to go back to the old-fashioned way of giving me directions. Neither of us could do anything but laugh at it. We both had a lot of fun, but the shoot did take much longer than had been anticipated.

To add to the equation of making things difficult, Rhian was to be in a few of the photos. As life would have it, she was not going to co-operate. It was 37 degrees Celsius, late in the afternoon, and she wasn't interested in staying still and posing like a glamour dog. There were too many interesting flies buzzing around to catch with her snappy mouth. I think the old saying about never working with animals or children needs to be 'never work with blind people and their dogs!'

Another issue with not being able to see the camera, or photographer for that matter, is holding the smile. It can be hard enough trying to retain a natural smile but when you're holding it for a long period of time and posing as well, it becomes very tiring. Here I am, all ready to go, thinking that the camera is clicking away, when the photographer is still setting up equipment and adjusting the lighting. Now I tell them to announce when they are prepared to start shooting so I am not looking like a grinning Cheshire Cat for hours on end, with a face ache to go with it!

At times, even Les forgets I can't see the camera. I asked him to take a couple of different photos that I needed. All dressed up once again, I explained to him the type of photo that was required. He kept telling me to look at the camera. I retorted back, 'Well, you need to give me some directions to where you are. I can't see, remember dear?' With a chuckle, he said, 'Sorry dear, sometimes I forget you're blind.' Typical male, I thought, selective memory when it suits them. I bet you wouldn't forget when it's dinner time, was the sarcastic thought in my head. Not only does he make those comments about trying to look at the camera, but then when he reviews the photos, he also tells me my smile is to put on and I look like a grinning monkey. Thanks, dear, for your kind and uplifting words!

That is when I have to just brush it off and laugh about it. Luckily, I am so self-confident and don't take things personally, but man, sometimes it's hard work trying to stay uplifted and bubbly about life when you're married to your inner critic!

Colleen Ashby

Playing blind canasta

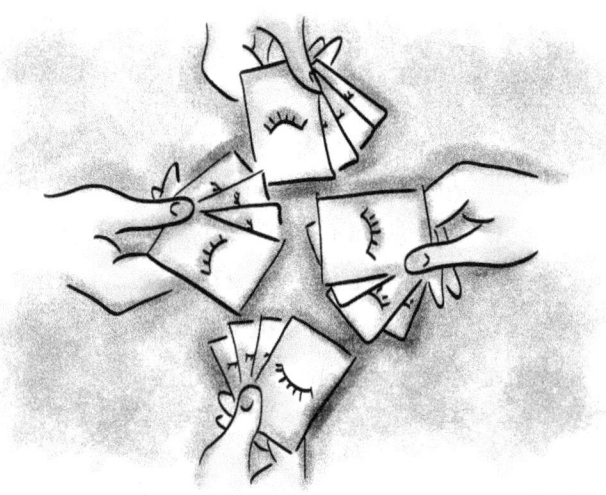

One true joy is playing canasta. For years, Hon and I have been swearing at one another with tremendous enthusiasm. These Tourette's-like outbursts are both uncontrollable and inevitable as the tension of the game evolves. Throw in another player, such as Sue (also known as Duchess), and the language and snide comments escalate to an even higher level! This brings about a noteworthy degree of fun and suspense.

It was in the second year after my transplant and having lost all but a fraction of my sight that Hon and I devised a way of returning to our mutual love and joy. Using the large playing cards, we combined canasta with samba (a more difficult variation of canasta). Changing the rules and taking out the lower point cards, we invented 'blind canasta.' Yes, we were back in a love-hate state for hours. Hon also has two close friends, Sean and Cindy, who loved playing canasta. Sean, Cindy and I had learned about each other in quite some depth through Hon, our mutual friend. I call them friends, even though I had never met them because I knew them quite intimately through Hon.

One day, while Hon and I were playing, she texted Sean, to tell him I had thrashed her. His witty comeback was, 'You let Helen Keller beat you? Don't you know you can cheat? She's blind, remember. She won't know!' Hon relayed this message and we were both in hysterics. She and I decided we needed to arrange a match for us all to meet and play 'blind canasta' together.

A meeting, over twenty years in the making, was finally arranged. I was excited about participating with Sean and Cindy in our mutually loved game. They were both a bit hesitant, with those frequently asked questions that arise when meeting someone with a disability. Hon reassured them I could take a joke and give back what I was dealt. 'Don't treat her any differently than you would me.'

When Hon introduced Sean and Cindy to me, I announced, 'Hi, my name is Keller. Helen Keller!' in a James Bond style of talking. With that, they relaxed, and the laughing immediately ignited. Sitting down at the table, I was opposite Sean. This meant he was the only one I really had to worry about as he could pick up the cards I threw out. Rules explained, we let the long-awaited match begin.

Quick witted remarks were flying out of Sean's mouth, directed at everyone at the table. It wasn't long before I started up with some explicit language and witty comebacks. Everyone was comfortable and at ease as the game got under way.

As I couldn't see what the opponent might have laid down in front of them, I had to keep asking them (Sean, in this matter) what they had before I discarded. Now, I am used to Hon telling me how many of each card she had down. When I inquired with Shaun if he had any eights down, he simply replied, 'Yes.' With the cards in my hand, I didn't have much choice in what else I could give him; they were all cards I needed to hold onto.

As I placed my eight down on the discard pile, Hon and Cindy immediately screamed out, 'Colleen, No!' This was followed by exasperated moans and sighs as Sean, grinning like a cocky little upstart who has just gotten away with thieving something, reached for my discarded card.

Not too sure what was going on, I asked Sean, 'How many eights do you have down?'

His cheeky short answer was, 'Six.'

'Yep, you just gave him a natural canasta,' Hon retorted.

Realising this was like sleeping with the enemy, I said, in a pissed-off manner, 'Sean! That's not fair. You're meant to tell me how many cards you've got down.'

'Well, you didn't ask,' was his smug comeback, delivered in an insolent but extremely humerous tone. 'You said you don't like being treated any differently, and so I'm not. That should make you happy.' That was it. Game on! I'll show you, trying to trump Helen Keller! Get ready, I'm coming after you mate. I managed to black three him six times in a row (black threes are useless cards as you can't do anything with them). This really pissed him off, and the witty and narky comments were flying around faster than a blue-ass fly at a barbeque. I was loving every minute of it. I may be Helen Keller, but I am very well equipped with great hearing, as well as a voice to express my annoyance.

I hate to say this, but he Helen Kellered me again a few rounds later! Bastard! But I knew his trick now and he wouldn't pull that one on me again. Well, at least I hoped not.

We all agreed it was the best and most fun game of canasta any of us had played. They loved the funny stories about my life since losing my sight, and we all enjoyed some ridicule and banter derived from love. It was a unanimous vote to all play again.

I know I don't like being treated any differently to anyone else but really, Shaun, surely there must be some form of lenience.

Colleen Ashby

It's all perspective

For over eight years I had supported children with special needs at school. I loved this work, getting to understand the children's behaviours and ways, hopefully making them feel safe and comfortable with me helping them. Life can be tough for these children as they generally find it difficult fitting in, both socially and academically, at school. My personal passion was students with autism and understanding their amazing, unique thinking. For anyone who is different and doesn't quite fit into that little 'socially acceptable' box, life can be cruel. I loved being a safe haven for these kids.

Now in the same job role but with no sight, the tactics of the game play needed to be adjusted, and that was fine, for that is how innovative ideas are created. All parties involved needed to make adjustments to make it work. This included the students.

Ya Gotta Laugh

So, here I was, having been absent for over a year, back in the classroom with a student I had been supporting for a couple of years prior. He was on the autism spectrum and needed quite intensive support. He had heard all about my health issues with the heart transplant and then losing my sight, so was extremely pleased to have me sitting by his side once again in the classroom. He told me how upset he was when he heard all about my near-death experience and then becoming blind, and how he was so relieved to see me again. He then leaned over to me and quietly said, 'You know, Mrs Ashby, you and me are the same.'

'How's that?' I curiously enquired.

'Well, we both have a disability. I have autism and you are blind, so we are the same,' was his proud response, as if we were now both on equal terms. Knowing the extremely black-and-white way of thinking these children often had, two of my sons are on the autism spectrum, I felt a funny feeling of joy and equanimity with this statement. There was a smile in my heart about this innocent and endearing way of seeing life.

I responded, 'You are absolutely right. We are the same. I help you with your autism and you can help me with my blindness by reading things to me and telling me what's going on.' As a neurotypical person, there would be no way I would equivalate my state of vision to being on the autism spectrum. He, however, could see the common factor of us both having a labelled disability. I felt the connection between us deepen, with a knowing that we had each other to cover our backs in times of need. It certainly goes to show you that everything is just a matter of perspective and the way we view life.

Colleen Ashby

Shopping in the perfume department

There is nothing like meandering slowly while looking through the perfume department. Imagine stopping to smell the beautiful scents as the accumulated fragrances waft through the air, creating a cherub-filled cloud from heaven; then trying the fragrances on until your olfactory senses get so overwhelmed they stop working. The very fragile and delicate arrangement of the beautiful displays on glass shelves brings in the visual aspect to add to the whole experience, enticing you to stay longer.

My first encounter with going into one of these departments since losing sight was when I had my cane. I entered alongside my girlfriend, with my cane rolling from side to side telling me if there were obstacles ahead. Once we were in there, we separated as she was lured away towards her favourite fragrance. I continued in the shop as if I knew where I was going, my cane hitting things as I went. Naturally wanting to be just like a normal customer browsing, I paused, about to pick up a bottle of perfume to smell, even though I had no idea what it was. A shop assistant in lightning speed came over, asking if I needed any help. Obviously, her brain was rolling through an imaginary movie of me knocking over the delicate and expensive glass bottles as my hands tried finding them, or worse still, of me turning around and bumping something, completely annihilating the carefully designed display.

I awkwardly fumbled out 'No, I'm just looking around, thank you.' She was reluctant to move far from my personal space, understandably concerned with her premonition of what calamity was possible, so I retreated from the perfumes. My friend was now aware of the shop assistant's dilemma and quickly came over reassuring the assistant that we were exiting this precarious situation. Luckily, I didn't do a Monty Python-esque performance of going into the perfume department waving my cane around in the air, obviously smashing everything in my scope, only to have the shop assistant come frantically running over, desperately asking if I needed any assistance. My casual and nonchalant reply would still have been 'No thank you, I am just looking around.' Now that would be funny!

Now you can see the apprehension from a shopkeepers' perspective when a blind person enters their place of livelihood. They obviously know they can't refuse them on an account of discrimination, but at the same time they are obviously concerned with what foreseeable disaster could occur, costing them money. I have shown you the response when I enter a shop with delicate products. Well, now imagine the increased angst from the owner or assistant when I walk in with Rhian!

Kitchen shops with glassware or those shops that have fine ware scattered throughout are high up there on the list of places where I raise the assistant's blood pressure and anxiety level. My most memorable experience was in a favourite crystal shop of mine. Full of beautiful glass cabinets filled with a rainbow of exotic and well sought-after crystals. There are also bowls around a circular stand where you can feel and pick up the crystals to check they are right for your energy. Once again, this shop is particularly crammed with goodies in a very limited space, so moving throughout it is quite a skill in itself. Not only do I have Rhian's harness, increasing our cumulative width, but her wagging tail also makes for an ideal bat to knock bowls and scatter crystals all over the floor.

Not so dangerous as in breakage concern, but it is stressful to think of ruining the displays in those shops that cram in so much stuff you can't even fit one person through the passageway. You know the ones. The stationery shops where as soon as you move, something falls down off the shelf.

I don't even notice when Rhian has accidentally knocked something down as we make our way through. It's only that people come quickly over, picking up after the destruction I have left in my wake! When I notice this, I will turn around, typically creating more demolition. I profusely apologise, but the response is always something along the line of 'No, don't apologise, it's fine. I will fix it in no time.' All the while, I am sure they are wishing for me to just exit the shop already!

It has taken me a few years to learn through experience what shops are viable for me to safely enter without causing stress for either the shopkeeper or myself. If I am with someone shopping, I will tell them that I am happy to just wait outside while they have a look around. Even though I have wonderful memories of once perusing these quaint beautiful shops filled with visual delights, I have come to the point where trying to do this now is not so easy. I can't really see what is on display anymore, but I remember loving looking through these stores. I have had to let go of that attachment and accept that when you lose sight of where you are going, some things need to change, and I'm okay with that now.

Colleen Ashby

Taking the final step

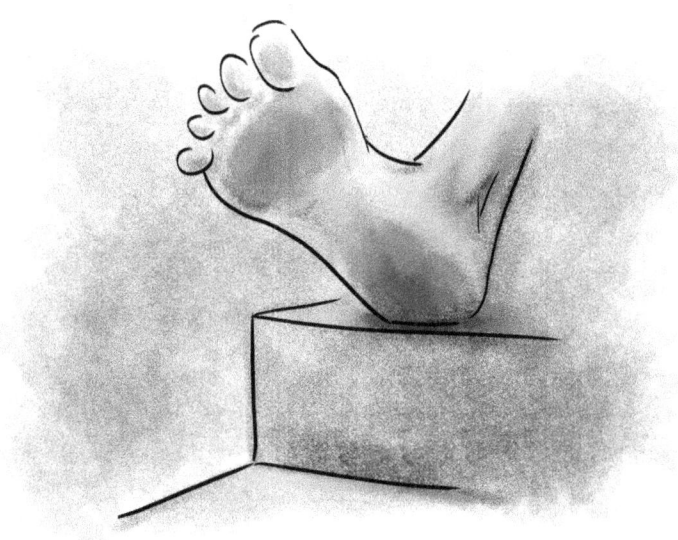

We have all heard a saying like 'taking a leap of faith' or 'taking the final step,' and it usually implies an emotional or personal concept of moving forward to attain a state of happiness, or deciding to finally go for a goal you haven't dared to achieve. Both these analogies are extremely important for one's personal and spiritual growth. It is only through endeavouring to expand oneself that limited personal boundaries are broken. Without this will to be something greater than ourselves, we wouldn't be able to experience the full magnificence and wonder of life. Well, that is not what this anecdote is about at all!

I am talking about literally or physically taking that final or bottom step. You wouldn't think about walking down a flight of stairs, would you? Only subconsciously taking notice of the width or depth of the step so you can prepare your body. You receiving messages in your brain through visual input and use your depth perception to tell your muscles to adjust your gait. Your vision will also alert your body when the ground levels out again. So, let's see how this task pans out when you take away your visual input.

My first practice with walking down steps was at home. I have a set that goes down to our backyard. They are lovely wide treads, twelve steps in all with a wide landing in the middle. Holding onto the limestone wall on the side, I counted six steps then paused on the landing. Feeling for the edge with my foot, I then counted a further six steps before landing on ground level. Going up is a lot easier to navigate but I still count my paces. Even today, as I proficiently walk down the back stairs, I still count them out in my head. I need to, or else I don't know where I am up to, and I still need to ready myself on the landing platform to prepare for the bottom section.

When it comes to a large flight of stairs in a public place, I will always use a handrail to support me, in case I misjudge the landing or bottom level. I will also tend to crab step down them if the tread of the step is narrow. I have learned to do this after experiencing a couple of good tumbles early on.

My favourite amusing memories are of when I would have friends guide me down a flight of stairs. For some bewildering reason, they would always like to count the steps right from the top one until we arrived at the landing. One of these staircases had 22 steps, so as I was hanging on to the handrail to steady myself, concentrating on where I was placing my foot, my brain was listening to someone methodically counting like they were watching a children's television program teaching them to count! Why they felt as if counting aloud helped me, I have no idea! The issue was that when it came time for the crucial information that I really needed, which was where the final step was, they never gave it to me, or they gave it too late! At times, I told them I didn't need them to count the steps for me but to make sure they informed me when the bottom level was next. On many an occasion, I thought I had arrived at ground level and proceeded to walk forward when splat! I would land like a ton of bricks on my knees, usually incurring quite some degree of pain, let alone the embarrassment of basically falling flat on my face!

I am extremely cautious now of assuming I am safely on ground level before striding forward. I would rather take my time and not rely on other people to tell me when to take that leap of faith forward from the last step. Too many confused conversations between myself and the other person of: 'Is this the bottom step?'

'No, one more step.'

Then, 'So, this is the ground level now?'

'Yep, you're on it now,' only to find that I would be on it next! It was quite comical, as this exchange was going on. For any onlooker, I am sure they would think we were performing a John Cleese sketch, especially if I managed to do a grand stunt of tumbling down the final step!

Ya Gotta Laugh

Technology and apps

If you had to lose your vision, the era that we live in now is the best time to have it happen. Advancements in technology have been truly amazing. Now there is an app for almost anything at your fingertips on your phone. There are devices to do just about any job you can think of that you would need to replace vision. I will go through just a few of the ones that I use frequently in my everyday living.

Beginning with apps on my phone, the most utilised one is called Seeing AI. This little beauty reads any print matter in its camera view. Hold the phone over an envelope, recipe or anything with print and it will read it out. The drawback to this is that it reads everything, and I mean *everything*. This aspect can become quite burdensome, as it reads the fine print on letters, including ABNs, email addresses, phone numbers and so on.

You must try and readjust the camera frame to just include the letter content, but is still a handy app. I use it all the time to read recipe cards or information sheets. Its other limitation is that it only reads black on white, so if you have a coloured background with a white or even black font, it can't read it. It also needs to be a flat surface, so trying to read a label on a can doesn't work.

Another handy app for when you are out and about trying to find a shop or restaurant is Blind Square. This works, like any navigation system, by entering your destination point to get directions, but it will also announce anything that is in your current vicinity. This lets you know what shop or building you are coming up to or passing. You set the range of distance and the building types you want it to announce. Very handy to have.

Not so much an app, but another utility on the phone is Voice Over, which you will find under the accessibility menu in Settings. This enables the phone to narrate everything you touch, like icons, plus it announces when you have a text message or any other notification you have turned on. It reads messages, emails, documents or any narrative you would see with your eyes. I have become super-efficient with Voice Over, listening with lightning speed, only needing the first few syllables to know what it is announcing.

The only thing you must remember is if you want to try this on your own phone, you need to learn all the hand gestures and commands to operate the device. If you don't, frustration will rise extremely quickly in your endeavour to keep operating it like normal (which won't work). I have learned all the tap and swiping combinations with the varying number of fingers to efficiently operate my phone. I can tell you though, early on I

Ya Gotta Laugh

found it extremely frustrating and thought I would never be able to learn how to operate it competently. A little word of advice: if you see someone listening to commands on their phone, please don't interrupt or talk while they are doing this. Listening to Siri as she says what needs to be heard is of the utmost importance. There is nothing more annoying than when I am trying to get information from Siri, and someone begins talking to me over the top of it. As I said before, you can only listen to the current announcement, and two lots of talking just doesn't work.

Believe it or not, but Siri is even extremely helpful when taking photos. Yep, she will tell you where the heads are in the picture frame and if it is level. Telling you to tilt left or right and then when it is straight. I love taking photos while people watch on and are boggled as to why or how a blind person would be wanting to take a photo. The ones that I do take, I get wonderful comments on what I have captured in the photo. I am not kidding either, they really are particularly good!

A device extremely useful for letting you know what items are is a barcode scanner. The inbuilt inventory is huge. Pick up the item, scan the barcode and it will announce what it is. Food, CDs, personal care, anything that has a barcode it has in its memory. If you want to label something yourself, say plastic envelopes or folders, you can do this too. A roll of spare barcodes comes with it, so all you do is stick it onto whatever you want, then you voice what you want to call it and when you scan it, your voice recording is announced. Pretty handy, don't you think? I really should use this device a bit more.

Document readers are also a handy tool to have. Quite a lot easier than the Seeing AI. This is like a scanner. You place the document or print matter on the screen, then once it is scanned, it reads it out to you.

In the kitchen department, there are a multitude of technologies available. The most recent one I obtained, which made the family extremely happy, was a talking thermometer. Now they don't have to eat raw chicken and get salmonella. Chicken, for some reason, I always manage to undercook, but now my trusty talking gadget tells me when it is done properly.

I frequently use talking scales and measuring jugs, along with my talking microwave.

The boys do find the microwave annoying at times, as it always announces when the door is open or shut, along with expressing whatever button you have pushed. Great if you were by yourself. At least you would have someone to talk to, although a little limited in conversation content. It's also a bit inconvenient when you want to do a sneaky heating-up of something in the middle of the night. When the house is dead quiet and you turn on the microwave, it certainly sounds like it has turned up its decibel level on purpose. I think it must have a secret program running as an informer or snitch. Not letting you get away with anything sneaky.

On appliances that don't talk, sticky or Velcro dots are placed on the appropriate settings. My oven has a dot on the grill point and then on oven. A dot also tells me where the 180 and 200 degrees points are. This way, I know how far to turn the knob. On my previous microwave, as well as the one at work, sticky dots were placed on the one-minute button, stop, and start. At least I could heat items up one minute at a time.

The same for my computer keyboard. There are bright coloured Velcro stickers on the main land points on it, so I can know where my fingers are more quickly. The main function keys are also dotted, making it simpler to navigate the keyboard.

I also have a mobile talking hotplate that can be used at home or when we are holidaying somewhere in a self-contained apartment. All these items lower the risk of getting burnt or starting a disaster in the kitchen. There is one item that I don't use, as it is annoyingly screechy. This liquid measurer is placed on the side of the cup and as you pour liquid into it, a squeal is emitted. Then when you top it up further, say milk in coffee, it lets you know you are at the top by releasing a screech like the owl in *Harry Potter* delivering a squealer letter. Not pleasant at all. That's why if you get a cuppa made by me it may only be three quarters full. Better than not having a drink at all, or worse, me spilling it all over the bench. Personally, I would advise you just accept it graciously and don't complain the tide is out. That way, we will both be ensured to remain happy!

There are a multitude of other devices to aid a person with no vision in getting around. These glasses have a tiny camera mounted on the side of the frame arm that is connected to an earpiece via bluetooth. It announces anything coming into the camera view, such as people, dogs, buildings, along with any print matter. You can adjust the range of information that you require, as it can become a case of information overload. I personally haven't gone down this track, but the option is there.

If you were blind, items very handy to have would be tiny sock pegs. These are designed to keep socks together in the washing machine and then when drying. After all, you wouldn't really want to be wearing odd socks out in public, would you? Unless that's your quirky way of being different. Not my style, though.

As you can see, there is just about an app or device for anything needing visual feedback. The one device I would love to have invented is something that makes putting plugs into power points easier. If you know any inventive people out there, pass on this challenge to them. It would be greatly appreciated by not only me but any other vision-impaired person, I am sure.

Ya Gotta Laugh

Identity classification

All of us identify ourselves in multiple ways. Labels, groups, job titles are just a few ways in which we do this. I'm a teacher, dancer, swimmer and mother, to name a few labels I identify with. Identities give us a sense of belonging to tribes or communities we choose to be part of. I now identify myself as part of the blind and transplant communities. Each community tends to have their own way of talking to one another as well. Let me show you what I mean.

As part of the blind tribe, we introduce ourselves to the level of vision we have and what mobility aid the person has.

'Hi, I'm Colleen. I am legally blind with no central vision and have a seeing eye dog, Rhian.'

'I'm Sally. I am totally blind and use a cane.'

Our level of vision is the identifying factor. The length of time one has been blind will generally come into the conversation as well.

Members of the transplant community get identified by the organ part they had transplanted. The first time I was introduced to this type of labelling was when I was at the Transplant Games. Standing poolside with one of my team members, she would tell me a person's name followed by their transplanted organ part.

'This is Sally, she's a lung,' or 'This is Erick, he's a kidney.'

At first, I found this rather strange, but I very quickly adapted to this labelling way of communicating with one another.

At social gatherings, it is still the name followed by organ part.

'Bob, lung,' or 'Sarah, liver,' is the tribal way of introducing oneself. I suppose it's curiosity to know what type of transplant one has had. It almost feels like a ranking order as well.

A lung or heart transplant would be classified as a top-ranking General. Hearts could possibly outrank lungs slightly, coming in at Colonel, with lungs being Major. Of course, this would depend on if it was a single or double lung, then the ranks may change. Livers would rank at Captain, slightly ahead of kidneys, which would be Lieutenant. However, a pancreas and kidney would rank above a liver and kidney. Other transplants such as cornea or bone marrow would rank somewhere around Warrant Officer. Non-transplanted people would classify at Private rank. This is only my fun and joking way to view things, as none of us would be sucking oxygen today if we hadn't received this precious gift of life, and no gift is more precious than another.

The hearts community takes this tribal communication and hierarchy placement one step further. When you receive your new heart, you are given a number and a distinguished badge that goes with it. These badges are worn with pride at any official transplant function. On our private Facebook page or whenever meeting newbies, we state our name followed by our heart number. This number represents what number transplant you were in Western Australia. Our number one (still very much alive) was done 27 years ago. I am number 174, and the current number is over the 200 mark now. If you forget your number, fellow hearts will quickly jump into action calling out for numbers and dates to try and place where you fit. Not much different than a roll call within the establishment. I was always forgetting my number! Quickly forgiven though, when I reminded them I couldn't read my badge number and most of the time couldn't remember where I had safely placed it away.

Every couple of years, the Western Australian transplant community have a getaway for a few days. A way of getting to meet other recipients and having a relaxed and enjoyable time together. Activities and outings are organised to build comradery and create new friendships. This event is always highly anticipated and looked forward to.

At this getaway, I went down to breakfast in the morning with Rhian by my side, along with Sharon (alias Hon). we entered the dining area to be seated. Hon, accompanying me for the weekend, didn't know anyone there. Of course, with me not being able to see or spot anyone I knew, we were both at a loss for where to sit. The organiser came over to us and said, 'Kidneys are at the table to the left, livers are to the right.' Then, scanning around the room, she announced, 'Ahh, hearts are sitting at the back table.'

With this, we walked down to the hearts table and said good morning, but the table was full, so Hon and I sat at a smaller table by ourselves. This turned out to be a blessing in disguise. At the table next to us was a lovely couple, the man who was a liver. With that, a heart and liver friendship was ignited, and we have stayed connected ever since.

When I tell people how we recognise or identify people, they find it amusing. It makes sense to me that this type of labelling fits. Think about what you identify with and the type of language or communication style you use. Most of us don't think anything about it, as it is simply the tribal way.

The biased and the unbiased

Since I have been matched up with Rhian, I have certainly experienced a broad spectrum of people and places that have a biased attitude. I have been surprised with interactions on both sides of this coin. Some are overwhelmingly helpful and will bend over backwards to make Rhian comfortable, whilst at the other end of this scale, I have felt angry and humiliated.

It's always better to get the negative aspect of things out the way first, I feel, then you can finish on a positive note. So, here we delve into the dark side of the human psyche.

My very first encounter was when I landed in Perth and was waiting with Brooke, the dog trainer, and needed to get a taxi home. A taxi pulled up and as soon as he saw I had a dog, began making up all the excuses as to why he couldn't take us, saying the taxi behind would be more comfortable. When I got into the taxi behind him, the driver, who had observed the whole scene, jovially greeted us. He was extremely helpful in getting us settled into the taxi. He too was angered by this attitude of discrimination, so took down the offender's plate number and reported him.

The next interaction the following day was at a petrol station. I walked in with Rhian as Brook followed me in. Now, (remembering I can't see) I promptly walked right up to the counter to pay when I heard Brooke's very stern and official voice telling him that I had every right to enter the shop as Rhian was an assistance animal and that if he refused me, she would report him and there would be a fine to pay! This was all an unexpected outburst to me, as I had no prelude of this man's attitude or what body language he had been displaying.

It wasn't until I got into Brooke's car that she explained. As soon as I entered the building with Rhian, he started waving his arms in the air, harshly pointing his finger to direct me out of his shop. All the while displaying a vexed expression, vigorously shaking his head from side to side. Once I knew this, I could just imagine this scene as very funny. Here is this man, wildly gesturing in this animated furious performance about having a dog in his shop. Meanwhile, oblivious to this irate person jumping around in front of me, I walk happily in with a smile on my face, ready to be served! When you put it like that, you really have to see the funny side.

Another time, I was going into a local café with Mum when the waiter rushed over to me as she realized I was about to enter. She asked me if I wanted a menu and said she would bring it to the table, which was outside the coffee shop. It was winter and not only cold but drafty as well. I told her I would sit inside and come up and order when ready. Then it began! 'Sorry but it is shop policy not to allow dogs into the shop,' she firmly stated.

I politely replied, 'Yes, but Rhian is a service dog and can go anywhere that I do, and that includes coffee shops.'

The waiter re-iterated, standing firmly in the doorway so I couldn't get in. 'I know but it is our shop policy to not allow dogs in!'

Now I was beginning to feel my frustration rising rather rapidly while still trying to keep this pleasant. I uncharacteristically countered back, 'I don't care if it's your shop policy! I am allowed in this shop with my dog and if you refuse me, I will report you and there is a fine!' This waiter, now torn between what her boss had told her and my threat of reporting them, anxiously told me she would just go to her boss and see what he said.

Returning quickly, she told us we could come in but had to sit right next to the door and away from the other tables. You can imagine by now that both Mum and I had quite a bitter taste in our mouths over this awkward and not particularly pleasant encounter, both wishing we had never gone there in the first place. So as Mum went up to the counter to order coffee, I, in my little defiant way, wanted to put my point across. I got up from that table in the draft of the door and proceeded to sit down at a table right in the middle of the coffee shop. The table next to me had six women happily chatting away to one another, and several other tables had people sitting at them too. Yep, this is where I would be sitting, I mulishly decided, and plonked myself down with Rhian. There, take that! Ha. Shop policy, my arse! Sorry, but that's what I felt.

Mum came back and sat down and to make matters worse, the waiter told Mum, 'It's just that dogs are dirty animals.' To this very day I have never returned to that coffee shop and have told numerous people about my distasteful experience.

I used to try and be polite in the beginning but after a multitude of these experiences, I have mastered a strategy to bypass this issue. If it is a place that doesn't require you to wait to be seated, I will just walk right in and get Rhian to find a seat before any interaction can occur. If I get the early inkling of hesitancy from a waiter at the front of the shop, I will take the lead and state, 'That's alright, I can find my own seat and will order when I am ready, thank you.' Then I will steadfastly make my own way in. This leaves them no option, as they wouldn't want to make a scene inside the shop with other patrons looking on.

There was one time when I went a bit overboard with my reaction to the restaurant's maîtres d', but I need to backfill the events that had unfolded earlier on to get me to this extremely fragile and highly worked-up state.

I was over in Sydney with Les and my three boys, Stephen, Scott and Mark. I was there for the finale of a television show I was part of. I had to go to the studio for a dress fitting and then we were meeting the boys to have the afternoon visiting Darling Harbour. Les and I returned to set out on our adventure, all excited being in Sydney for a few days and of course going on the television show. My enthusiasm and vibrant vibe rapidly dissipated like a lead balloon when I saw the state Stephen was in. Extremely intoxicated. When he is in this state, his behaviour is loud and obnoxious with what he thinks is funny. There were numerous events along the way to Darling Harbour, but the tipping point soon came. He discovered the submarine his father was on years ago, sitting in the water of the Maritime Museum. Even though it was all closed off for the evening and had barricades around to stop people from venturing in, Stephen had this grand idea of jumping on his dad's submarine. I kept on walking and told the rest of the family that we didn't know him and to keep on moving. Then Stephen started bellowing out for Scott to take a photo. Next minute Stephen went running past us, briefly stopping to announce that security was chasing him. Then off he fled like a streaker being chased across a football field.

Now we were all left there with no idea where Stephen had gone. The men all set off in three different directions to try and find Stephen but all to no avail. I told Mark to phone him, but he told me Stephen had left his phone back at the hotel as it was flat. I then told Mark that Stephen could catch a taxi back to the hotel by himself, but Mark replied that Stephen didn't have any money on him. 'Great!' I announced. Here was Stephen with no phone, no money and most probably too drunk to even know where our hotel was. So, what the hell do we do now? As you can most probably imagine, tears were running down my face. Not only with concerns about that day's drama but of what he would be like when he was at the studio the next day in the audience. Les made the decision for us to just have some dinner and work it out later. On our way through the many bars and restaurants looking for a nice one to dine at, suddenly Stephen popped out from nowhere, all laughter and having a grand old time about the whole event. By now I was absolutely livid and at my wit's end with him. I told him not to even speak to me and just shut the f**k up! (Which he didn't, as he couldn't see anything but funniness about it).

We stopped at this restaurant where the maître d' greets you and finds a table to seat you. I asked for a table for five, picking up the menus and pointing to a table at the back, when he looked down and saw Rhian. Now it began. 'Sorry Ma'am, but it is our shop policy not to allow dogs inside.' You have got to be f**king kidding me! Not the bloody shop policy bullsh*t line again. Venom was now festering up inside of me, charged with all the emotions of the day with Stephen, and this maître d' was going to be the whipping boy. Not being able to contain myself any longer, the volcano erupted and the devil inside of me unleashed a wrath from hell!

'I don't care about your shop policy! Rhian is a working dog and can go wherever I go. She has flown on a plane all the way from Perth this morning. She is staying in the hotel with me. She goes on the train and in taxis and she is allowed to go into this restaurant if I want to go in here!' The maître d', now a little shaken by my unjustified and a bit extreme outburst, said we could sit here in the front area but not inside. Then I frustratedly snapped back, 'Forget it, I am not sitting here,' and stormed off with the family sheepishly following behind, I think too scared to say anything at all, with the state I was in. This was the first time the family had seen me in this furious state. It even shocked me, my public outburst, but I was feeling like a donkey on the edge.

Les then said, 'This place looks alright, do you want to try this one?' The new maître d' came over and grabbed some menus, then happily, showed us to a table right in the middle of this bustling restaurant, before getting us all seated and bringing a water bowl over for Rhian. We all had a pleasant meal once my emotional state settled, and the waiter even asked if Rhian was allowed a treat.

I know my outburst at the previous restaurant was emotionally fuelled and it was, unfortunately, an undeserved tongue-lashing for the poor maître d' just doing his job, but what a difference from one place to another.

To put things into perspective and balance the books of the biased and the unbiased, I will shine a light on the more common, pleasant and accepting demeanour of the human psyche.

The majority of places I go to with Rhian will always offer her a bowl of water and accommodatingly work around her. I was in one café that allowed dogs on the outside tables, even supplying a multitude of dog beds for them to lie in. Les and I were actually inside the café, but the waiter insisted that she get a nice soft comfy bed for Rhian and brought it inside for her to lie in. The best story was when I was in the hospital having a procedure done, which meant Mum had to sit in the waiting room for about an hour holding Rhian.

Well, when I came back, Rhian was not only extremely excited to see me again, but she had a hospital blanket on the floor, along with a plastic container filled with water. Mum told me ever since I was out of sight, Rhian had been whining. A doctor came out and thought she needed a nice warm blanket to lie on. Then a nurse decided she must need some water, and another even offered to take her for a walk. I think she got better treatment than the patients. Now that makes a whole lot of difference, when Rhian is well received and accepted as part of my life. That does make me incredibly happy, as it means the devil inside of me has no reason to come out!

Ya Gotta Laugh

Getting the lens right

On my return to working at the high school, Vision Australia gave me some props to use as an awareness task for the students. A range of cardboard glasses with plastic lenses made to show what the several types of eye conditions looked like. Macular degeneration, diabetic retinopathy and glaucoma were some of the disease lenses given to me. The idea is for people to put the glasses on and experience what it would be like seeing only what someone with that condition must deal with. Fantastic idea, I thought, especially for the younger students. It could be an interactive and fun task.

Janine, a fellow education assistant and dear friend, helped me in getting the lens right to suit my limited vision. Handing me a pair of cardboard glasses, she asked if that was how much vision I had. I told her it was good, and she then placed them on her own head. She asked me if I could see the pen on the desk. I told her no. 'Well, I can, so I will have to put some whiteout on the lens to obscure the vision more,' she announced.

Giving them back to me, she asked how that lens was now. Once again, I replied, 'Yep, that's perfect.' Janine took them back to put on again and asked me if I was able to see an object that was sitting on my desk shelf. Obviously answering no once more, she told me that she still could, so more whiteout needed to go onto the lens.

It never occurred to either of us, by giving me the glasses would be no help, as I was unable to see things anyway, so a true indication wouldn't be found by my say so. I forgot I couldn't see, and I suppose the same went for Janine. Both of us were still living in the reality of me being sighted. I could have placed a pair of clear glasses on and told someone, 'Yep, that's what my vision looks like!'

It was a huge laughing matter as we worked out there was no point in giving me the glasses to try on. Janine just kept slapping more whiteout on until she could only see a sliver of things on the right side.

The idea worked well with the students. As they looked around the room and at their books, it helped them to understand what it would be like to have limited vision.

Ya Gotta Laugh

The blind leading the blind

Once I had finally got my clearance to return to working in the high school I was relearning how to do things again with the support of a tutor. My brain quickly went into overload and had a total meltdown! I had to learn the commands with a software program that speaks everything to you, including every key stroke. To begin with this can seem quite overwhelming but within a brief time, your hearing becomes your eyes and listening intently becomes the norm. Anyone walking in and hearing the incessant babble coming from the computer would think it was artificial intelligence on steroids and the only way it had of expressing its built-up energy was to ramble on relentlessly, at quite some speed, without taking a breath. A computer with verbal diarrhoea, try and imagine that! So, as you can most probably imagine, having a nice quiet, uninterrupted space is high up there on the list of necessities. Not only is the computer talking to you but so is the tutor, telling you what to do, plus your own brain is chatting away, screaming at you that this is all too damn hard! I was certainly very relieved when I learned the command to be able to shut Siri up! I can tell you now, that is one command I made sure I never forgot.

By the end of the two-hour session, I felt I had forgotten everything I had learned. A total and huge brain fart (although a politically incorrect term, it is a perfect expression to describe the state I was in, and would stay in for the rest of the afternoon). Nothing was coming in or out of my brain. The fart was an all-encompassing empty hollow of air in my head. Luckily, they don't smell like ordinary farts!

Now to set the scene one step further, my tutor was totally blind. Why is a blind person tutoring another blind person? They have been through this whole experience themselves and have come out the other side fully competent and able to pass on their knowledge. It certainly astonished me at first when I learned the tutor was blind, but thinking about it, it really does make perfect sense. Getting back to my story, now that you know there are two blind people working together.

At first Manny, my tutor, had a support colleague come and help get me set up and introduce him to me. After the second week, when Manny would get to the school reception, they would just ring and tell me they were about to walk Manny down through the school to where I was. Knowing my way easily around the school, I told them I would come up and get him. Now, it was just at the end of the lunch break and all the students were still out in the grounds when I would come and bring Manny down the school pathway, through the grassed area and verandas. Manny would walk on my left, holding my elbow so I could lead him. He'd be tapping his white cane from side to side in front of him. And I'd be with my bright, hot pink cane with purple ball, rolling it from side to side as well, chatting along merrily as we went. One could almost imagine a scene like Ginger Rogers and Fred Astaire doing a dance sequence with canes. I could not see the students' faces, or the teachers', who were also watching in either amusement or bewilderment, but I certainly would have loved to have seen their expressions. Now, if that is not a case of the blind leading the blind, I don't know what is!

Colleen Ashby

The warmth of a fireplace

There is nothing like the natural soft warmth you get from a wood fire. It warms not only the air, but the whole building. When I was in Melbourne getting Rhian, Les and boys thought it would be a lovely surprise to put in a slow combustion fireplace for me. Right in the midst of Winter, nothing could be more welcome. Both the dogs loved lying right in front of the hearth, absorbing as much heat as they could. Let alone the humans lining up to heat our bottoms, standing close until we reach that fine line between pleasure and pain as our bottoms and legs begin to burn, and suddenly the heat is unbearable, so we have to step away.

At first, the menfolk wouldn't allow me to put any wood on the fire, concerned with the risk of burning myself. However, as time went along, that wall of concern began to crumble. After receiving a few good burns on my arm from putting the wood in, Les bought me some long protective gloves. Problem solved. The other issue that Les found was the burn holes in the lino flooring. Obviously, I couldn't see when pieces of coal or embers fell out of the fireplace, hence the damage to the flooring. A small price to pay for the lovely warmth we received from this wonderous black box.

Moving forward a year, I was confidently keeping the fire going along with utilising its other fantastic abilities, such as drying clothes, especially socks. The men's work socks take forever to dry, even in a tumble dryer, but put them on or around the fireplace and presto! They dry in no time at all.

I loved my newfound hobby of alternating between laying the socks across the front of the hearth and laying them on top of the combustion plate. I would merrily rotate them like sausages on a barbecue. The only issue with this process was if I got distracted with another task, the socks (much like sausages) would get a crispy skin. Sometimes Les would call out that he could smell something burning and I would frantically race over to the socks cooking on the fireplace then yell back, 'No, it's all right, dear, the socks are just drying. They're nearly done.' It wouldn't be until Les went to put his socks on that he would discover holes in them.

Deciding that drying socks on top of the fire was too dangerous, not only in respect to destroying socks but also in terms of the eminent risk of burning down the house, I agreed not to do it. I no longer utilised the hearth area for drying but draping socks over the wood holder would be a safe choice. Les, relieved, agreed this was a much better idea.

Obviously, the fire needed stoking up through the night and I was always up and down to the toilet, so I didn't mind doing this little chore. Then one morning, Les was looking for his other sock that had been drying on the wood stack. I reassured him it was definitely there last night. Then he noticed the glass of the combustion box. It had a black melted blob stuck to it. Opening the door, he saw half the sock still draped on the piece of wood and the other half melted onto the glass! I clearly picked up the piece of wood and never realized the sock was on it. So, we no longer dry socks on the wood pile either!

Ya Gotta Laugh

There is nothing wrong with my hearing

They say when you lose one of your senses, the others become heightened to compensate. At first, I couldn't decide if I thought that statement was true. What actually occurs is, you now tend to focus in on the other senses to help navigate your surroundings. Whether your hearing actually improves I couldn't personally say but my take on it is, your focus or awareness of sounds is heightened. In any case, I agree that my hearing is more focused and now alerts me of sounds from a further distance away than before.

I can be sitting with Les in the afternoon having a cup of tea when I will announce one of the boys is home. He will look out and check the drive or carport and say, 'No, they're not.' I will say, 'Yes, they are.' Then, a minute later, one of them will pull up into the carport. I can now hear them when they are up on the corner of the road, a hundred meters away.

Les finds it rather annoying as I catch him out when he tries to sneakily raid the pantry. We can both be sitting on the lounge watching television at night when he takes the empty cups of tea into the kitchen. You need to remember the sound of the television is still going, and the kitchen is on the other side of a brick wall, when I yell out, 'You don't need it, dear!' I can hear the slightest rustle of paper or the clink of the glass lid on the jar that contains sultanas. He thinks I have supersonic hearing now! He will come back like a guilty child who has sneaked a chocolate from the box. He always questions me on how I knew he was doing it. And I always reply that I can hear the rustle or clink of the jar. In fact, I hear a lot more of the slightest sounds now. Les feels like I am always watching over him with everything he does (that is, sneaking foods he knows he shouldn't be eating), like my hearing is the observing sniper who can take anyone out at quite some distance. I tend not to say anything anymore. I know he is doing it and he knows I know, but let's face it, nobody likes being caught out. At times, I imagine myself as Daredevil's secret identity, but when it comes time to perform the stealthy martial art moves with lightening quick reflexes and take out the villain, my persona would dismally fail. The hearing aspect of this superhero, though, I really can identify with.

The other aspect Les finds a little inconvenient is the volume of the television. Sounds seem so much louder now for me, and I am extremely uncomfortable with constant loud noise. It really makes me edgy, and I prefer to leave the room and find a quieter space in the house. He now puts subtitles on, so when we are watching television together, he can read what's being said. Between you and me, it most probably doesn't help that perhaps he is becoming a bit deaf, but we won't go there, alright?

I want to share an encounter that both my friend Deb and I thought funny. Please don't think that I am making fun of innocent bystanders and their perception of coming across a vision-impaired person. This is definitely not my intent, but some things are just plainly humorous.

Deb and I had just finished eating lunch at a busy restaurant. I told her I would just wait at the door while she went in to pay, sometimes when you are in busy and crowded places with a dog in harness, it is just easier to wait out of the way. So, standing in the doorway with Rhian at my side, I could tell there was a man standing to the right of me and not moving. I was beginning to feel a little uncomfortable with his presence, intently ogling me in curiosity. Deb finally came up behind me saying we were ready to go when this gentleman leaned over my shoulder and asked her, 'Is she blind?' Now to me it is a little bit obvious that someone standing in a doorway with a seeing eye dog and not making eye contact with anyone would obviously have some sort of vision impairment. Not only that, but to ask Deb over my shoulder, absurdly thinking that because I couldn't see I must have not been able to hear either! Deb, quickly saw the very funny John Cleese type of scenario that was occurring, leaned forward and said in a jovial but deriding tone, 'Yes, but there is nothing wrong with her hearing!'

Once this seemingly distressful disability was confirmed for him. He bent forward and empathetically repeated, 'Bless you, bless you, bless you,' as we walked off, chatting and laughing.

As I told you earlier, I am not making fun of this poor man, who was obviously extremely distressed to see someone who could not see, but surely it is not that bizarre to come across a blind person. I guess it may be difficult for people to understand that even though you may have lost a sense, that doesn't mean you can't do things in life. I do understand that, as I would most probably think the same way, asking myself about how one in this position would get on in life. It is still a funny little anecdote to share all the same.

One more encounter we still laugh about was when I was with my cousin Sharon. We were in a café waiting for our takeaway food. As we stood to the side of the counter and waited, Rhian, in harness, lay down. A man in his twenties excitedly came up to us, overjoyed and brimming with enthusiasm at seeing a seeing eye dog in a shop. He eagerly blurted, 'Is that a blind dog?'

Hon and I looked to each other smiling, trying to hold back the laughter that was busting to erupt, and said, 'The dog is not blind, but Colleen is.' We knew what he meant, and to see his bubbling excitement over Rhian was just gorgeous. In his excited animation, he couldn't find the correct words to express what he had meant. I then kindly said, 'Rhian is my seeing eye dog, to help me get around.' Once more we walked away having a quiet chuckle about the ridiculously cute event.

Ya Gotta Laugh

Comparing the market

This chapter is a continuation of the question about Rhian's total devotion or separation anxiety. It is not until you have a comparison of something that you are able to see things for what they really are. It's so easy to take for granted the idea that the way things are is normal and how they are meant to be. I have just recently had the opportunity, while participating in a cooking class with Vision Australia, to compare the market of seeing eye dogs.

Yes, Rhian was up against a brand new model fresh from the factory floor, with only four months of handling time. Instructional programming still untampered with, learning the handler's habits and ways. Will Rhian shine through with her four years of experience on this new, sleek black model, or will the latest technology outshine her? Place your bets, ladies and gentlemen.

Arriving at the cooking class, both of us handlers had a cooking bench for the dog to lie under. The dog, once told where to lie, is meant to stay there until told otherwise. The new model did exactly that. Lay down and didn't budge for the entire time, not even lifting her head when her handler left the bench. This amazed me, awaking me to the obvious fact that Rhian had never done this.

When we students had to go up to the front bench to observe the techniques and procedure we would be doing next, did Rhian stay under her bench? Nope! She followed me up to the front and stood by me. Even when I needed to walk to the sink to clean dishes, Rhian followed me all the way. It was then obvious to me that this needed some attention and a plan to try and remedy it.

The following week, I decided to tether her to the bench leg so she couldn't wander around behind me. Meanwhile, the Miss Goody Two Shoes new model just rubbed it in my face, showing her superiority over my older model by calmly lying unmoved all day under her bench! I wasn't going to have this upstart new kid on the block show up Rhian. I mean, after all, Rhian has flown on many planes, been on a television show like a movie star, plus worked in a high school. So beat that!

Well, my tethering idea was a dismal failure. She not only tried to drag the table to enable her to be near me, but she also whined if somebody stood in front of me blocking her view! As soon as I told them to step sideways so she could see me, she stopped whining. They were of course very amused at her behaviour and found it extremely cute. It is not only the issue of her even needing to see me all the time, but she never settles or relaxes during the entire time. Meanwhile, Miss New Model is sound asleep in doggy dreamland.

I persisted the next week again with the tethering idea, only to realise her desperate need to be with me. I was washing my dishes, well out of sight, when I heard the others talking to Rhian. Saying, 'It's all right, she'll be back soon. Poor Rhian, it's okay, don't stress.' They then called out to me, saying Rhian was whining and missing me. If that wasn't enough, the teacher thought she had done a wee on the floor. Thankfully, it was only water. Rhian had dragged the table leg and spilled the water bowl on top of the bench in her undying endeavour to be with me.

Reluctant to let this go on any longer, I told the teacher I will let her off and just let her follow me. Agreeing that this was a good idea, Rhian trailed behind me to the sink. Watching what I was doing, she simply lay down on the mat near the door and calmly stayed there until I went back to my cooking area.

I have come to accept that the new well-trained model isn't necessarily better than Rhian. It's simply a matter of understanding the strong connection and bond that she has with me. I for one, would never want to trade that for anything! She performs all her other tasks proficiently and I feel safe with her guiding skills. I think that is more important than being able to lie still under a bench all day.

Colleen Ashby

Toothpaste

Cleaning teeth is such a simple task we all learn to do right from when we are toddlers. Everyone cleans their teeth without even thinking about it. It is one of those habits where we don't even have to pay any attention to the process, right? Well, all I can say is, take the sense of sight away and one must restructure how to perform those habitual everyday practices.

Try doing it with your eyes shut! Not so easy and straight forward when you are trying to put the tooth paste on the toothbrush.

When I was first home after my transplant and having lost my eyesight, initially, Les would not say anything. However, a few weeks later, he came and said to me, 'I see you've cleaned your teeth, dear?'

'Why, what's the matter?' I responded.

'There are big blobs of toothpaste all in the basin. Not to worry, I'll clean it up,' Les replied.

'I was wondering why I seemed to be squeezing out toothpaste quite a lot but not getting any on the toothbrush,' I stated.

'I can see that, dear. That's why there are great globules of toothpaste all around the basin all the time,' he ragged.

'Well, you try and get the white toothpaste onto a toothbrush, which is also white, that you can't see to line up with, let alone over a white basin where you can't distinguish where a white blob of toothpaste may have fallen. I am too busy trying to work out if I managed to get it on the toothbrush, not thinking that blobs have fallen all around the basin. I wondered why even after I seemed to be squeezing the tube of toothpaste a lot, half of the time when I clean my teeth in the shower, it feels a bit dry and like not much toothpaste is on my brush!' I defensively countered back.

Now we usually try and get the striped coloured toothpaste but even with my miniscule bit of vision I have out of the corner of my right eye, I still have a tough time trying to see it. I have now started to run my hand around the basin and wipe any globules of toothpaste that have fallen.

The simple things we all take for granted, without even thinking about what we are doing in an autopilot mode. Take the sense of sight away and autopilot functions certainly begin to glitch

Besides having a basin that looks like a flock of seagulls have flown over it (and on the bench, as well but I'm letting that one slide), there is another ramification that can occur without sight. That is, obviously, not knowing what things are when they're in tubes and bottles.

When I was in hospital, they gave me a personal hygiene pack which contained three tubes. One was shampoo, another conditioner and the third body lotion. All of these were in exactly the same tubes, except for the differences in the writing on them. I would have to ask the nurse which one was which before I had my shower. Normally, at home I always buy shampoo and conditioner that are in differently shaped bottles, to tell them apart. Another handy item that was in this pack was a toothbrush with a tiny tube of toothpaste. I thought it was ridiculously cute. Naturally, once I was home, I put this toothpaste in the bathroom cupboard in case of the emergency of running out.

Quite some time later we did happen to run out of toothpaste so, remembering this, I went into my bathroom cupboard to retrieve it. Upon successfully finding it, I proudly placed some on both Les and my own toothbrush, quite chuffed I was able to resolve this toothpaste dilemma, I proceeded to clean my teeth. Les coming in a little later to do his teeth, commented on the funny tasting toothpaste which didn't froth up like normal. I thought there was a slight difference in flavour but didn't give it much thought. Les wiping his mouth after cleaning his teeth, once more remarked on the strange and not particularly pleasant toothpaste.

Ya Gotta Laugh

I came into the bathroom to reassure him that it was the little hospital toothpaste and showed it to him. As he read the label questioningly to me, I immediately took a step back, aghast and somewhat humiliated. This paste was certainly meant for an orifice, but not the one we put it into! It was for fungal issues that women commonly get downstairs, in the ladies' lingerie department. Les didn't know how to respond, knowing now what he had just lathered throughout his mouth. I chuckled, stating, 'Well, I guess we won't have any fungal issues going on in our mouths!'

Colleen Ashby

Mistaken identity

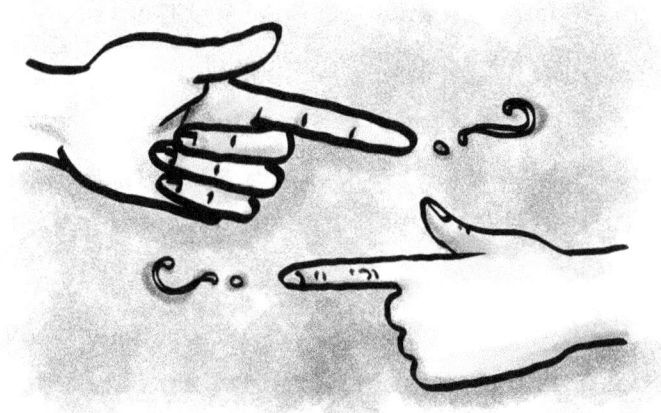

Les and I were at a meeting where competitors for the Australian Transplant Games were gathering to order uniforms and get to meet one another. It was held at an independently owned hamburger place where there was plenty of room to sit together. Once the introductions were done and uniform formalities were completed, food could be ordered to be eaten while we socialised with one another. This was all new to me as I had only been transplanted six months earlier, so was classified as a newbie. Everyone was extremely friendly, especially with word getting around about me having lost my vision from the transplant, and I was made very welcome.

Lining up to order our food, Les and I were chatting away to other team members, having a laugh and exchanging stories. Getting closer to the counter, I leaned closer into Les and began talking to him. Asking what he was going to order and could he read me the menu to choose from. A voice then answered me, 'I can certainly read you the menu.'

I stepped back and stated, 'You're not Les?' in a jovial but embarrassed way. We both began to chuckle over this harmless but slightly uncomfortable situation.

The man then yelled out to Les, 'You had better come over before your wife wants anything more from me besides some help ordering food!'

Others hearing this debacle soon roared laughing and jokes around the room were firing off everywhere. Les was getting slaps on his back for allowing his wife to try and make off with a strange man, as he quickly moved up a few positions in the queue from where he had stopped to chat to other members, obviously forgetting all about me. All the while, thinking I was with Les, I had been gabbing away to this gentleman. Not only talking to him but leaning right up close and personal, so he could hear me with no issues.

At least this gentleman knew I couldn't see and so was extremely obliging with his humorous response, and as for Les, he knows he can't leave me alone in a room full of strangers as God only knows who I may be chatting up and walk off with! It's a real example of the saying, 'I can't leave her alone for five minutes.' No, you sure can't, dear!

Another case of mistaken identity is when my boys come home from work on a Monday, which is Mark's TAFE day for studying his mechanic apprenticeship. I will begin chatting away to him as if he were Scott. From a distance, the only way I can tell them apart is because Mark always wears shorts and

Scott long trousers. Both being the same height and wearing the same work shirt, they look exactly the same with what vision I have. Seeing one of them walk in with long trousers, I naturally assume it is Scott, forgetting Mark has to wear long trousers for TAFE. Then he responds, 'It's me, Mum, not Scott!' I apologise, feeling bad about not being able to tell them apart from a distance. Mark naturally makes some joke about it. I am sure they understand, but it still makes me feel awkward, viewing myself as a bad mother, unable to tell my children apart.

Another common case of mistaken identity is when we are at the dog beach. As you can imagine, there are numerous dogs of all shapes and sizes but at the same time there are quite a few black dogs. Throwing the frisbee for Rhian, there are often several other canines all eager to retrieve it for her. Most of them halt at the water, while Rhian leaps over the waves and boldly ventures out to where other dogs fear to swim. When she returns triumphantly onto terra firmer, the other canines gather around her, admiring this Sporty Spice dog, I think wishing they were as courageous as this canine female warrior! Amidst the bustle of dogs, I bend down to pat Rhian, only to have Les tell me that it is not her, she is further down the beach. I don't feel quite so inept about this mistake, as black dogs to anyone could quite possibly look the same. Well, that's what I think, and I am sticking to it.

Not so much a case of mistaken identity, but it is an issue I face of confusion over who I am talking to. This was a frequent occurrence until I was taught how to position my head correctly. Having only five percent vision out the corner of my right eye, I naturally turned my head about 45 degrees to the left to capture what vision I could of the person I was talking to. To me this seemed the right thing to do. As far as I was concerned, I was making eye contact with them, which was the socially acceptable thing to do. I never realised my head was tilted so far past the person I was addressing, I never even gave it a thought. Talk about mixed messages!

I was helping with a large group of students in the high school and my job was to hand out these wristbands to the students. Two girls were standing together waiting, chatting to one another. I looked at the girl on my right and asked if she wanted to come over and get a wristband. I saw her turn her head to her friend on her right (my left) in a querying manner, then turn back to me. confirming her query, I said, 'Yes, you.' She again turned to her friend, who was pointing her finger back to herself, gesturing to ask if it was her I meant. I was completely misunderstood like I was speaking another language, repeating, 'Yes, you.' Now both girls were completely bamboozled as to who I was talking to, pointing fingers at themselves and then to each other! I of course did not realise I was looking to the student on my left. As far as I was concerned, I was looking directly to the girl on my right! Realising this whole conversation had been lost in translation, I pointed to the girl on my right and repeated, 'You.' As she nodded her head, with a sigh of relief I pronounced, 'YES, you on the left!'

Finally stepping towards me, I gave both girls a wristband as we giggled about the miscommunication. That was a very awkward moment for me, as it made me realise how vital eye contact can be in making communication fluid and understood.

It was two years after that event that a physio pulled me up on it. I was having pain with structural issues from always adjusting my head to the left to utilise what sight I had. I told her I also did it to make eye contact with the person with whom I was engaging. She explained that where I was always looking was directly past that person's right shoulder, so they would be wondering what was so interesting over there where I was focused. She told me to practice looking directly ahead when talking to people. One, for my structural issues and two, so that who I spoke to would actually feel like I was engaging with them. I still find it hard doing this, as when I look directly ahead, all I see is a dark grey blank wall of nothingness, and I like to make eye contact when I talk to someone. I wonder if I will ever get used to interacting this way.

Another family member who now receives mixed messages is our pet dog Jasper. I didn't know my sight (or lack thereof), would have such an effect on animals but alas, it certainly seems that way.

Jasper would always jump up on my lap when I gave him a quick glance and a nod of my head, saying, 'Come on then,' with my hands open. With no hesitation, he would do a flying leap and then snuggle on my lap. Now, however, I can open my arms and say the words to come on up while looking at him (well, as far as I am concerned, which we all now know is not so the same as far as others are concerned) and he will just sit there. Slapping my hands on my lap and announcing the command to come up, this time with a louder and somewhat frustrated voice, he still would just sit there! I will have to turn on my stern commanding voice for him to finally relent and jump up. Giving him a snuggly pat and cuddle, he will nestle down in my lap.

The other frustrating thing for Jasper is when he is outside and the dogs want to follow me in. Rhian is quick off the mark and hot on my heels, following promptly behind me. Meanwhile, Jasper, somewhat of a dawdler, casually swaggers behind. I have to hold the self-closing door open for him, whilst telling him, 'Come on,' but he just stands still and waits! I look directly at him, but of course we know that's not quite the truth and Jasper is also in on this secret, so he is reluctant to make his move. Again, I will have to bring out my big voice, telling him to 'Come on!' He hesitantly makes his way forward before pausing at the doorway once more to look up at me, and only then will he proceed through, still at a dawdle, I may add.

When I first relayed this behaviour to Les, he told me that on several occasions after I had walked through the door with Jasper following, I had guillotined him in the heavy sliding door. 'AHH! I never knew that,' I replied.

Now I know that poor little Jasper is simply preserving his own life from being finished off by the guillotine sliding door, and he sees me as the executioner! So I wait patiently for him to take his time coming inside the house.

Colleen Ashby

Playing the blind card

I have been in quite a dilemma as to whether I should add this story in. It does not exactly reach too high on the moral code of conduct. It might make my life's directional compass start swinging frantically between either side of the true moral point. I thought, though, if I was going to be totally open and honest, I needed to add it in. I am doing this more for myself, to relieve my guilty conscience, as a Catholic would use a confessional box to redeem their sins. Well you, my friends, are my priest. So, get ready to bless me and tell me to do five Hail Mary's and then I am good to go to heaven.

In the early months after losing my sight, my girlfriend picked me up to go to a shopping centre. After our little shopping expedition, it was time to re-energise with a caffeine fix.

This coffee shop had a membership card to get benefits, but you had to pay an annual subscription. Getting out her membership card, my friend realised it was out of date by a couple months. She hesitated as to whether she should try and use it, so I quickly stepped in with a solution. I told her to give me the card, stand behind me and let me do the talking.

Stepping up to the counter to order, I told the cashier what I wanted and then handed the card over. Upon putting the membership number into the till, she announced that it had expired. I began acting out the performance of a lifetime.

'Oh, is it? I am sorry, I wasn't aware. I had a heart transplant four months ago and lost my sight from it. I'm not up to sorting these sorts of things out at the moment. I will have to get someone who can see to help me fix it,' I apologetically replied. Now the poor women, with this sob story, felt her heart strings pulled twangy tight and reassured me it was quite all right, she would just put it through with the discount this time and not to worry about it.

The performance was wildly enhanced by the fact that I obviously didn't make eye contact and fumbled quite a bit as I paid with my card, missing the correct spot and asking for her help to do it. Yes, performance superbly acted!

If this wasn't enough, my friend and I were back there the following fortnight. Luckily, my friend told me it was a different server. I told her to once again give me the card and stand back. I approached the counter with my hot pink cane.

I heard the same announcement about the membership not being valid. My performance was even more polished this time, with more fumbling around and apologising about the situation. You would have been applauding me with my believable act. I almost produced tears with my story. Seeing my glassy eyes, she comfortingly told me to get it sorted out for next time and that she would still put the discount on.

My friend and I were holding in the raptures of laughter. Getting away with this a second time was quite a task. Once we were sitting at a table, we had a good but quiet joke about my rendition. My moral justification with having done this was that there had to be some kind of payoff or benefit for losing my sight. I needed to use it to my advantage when possible. I told her, 'I call it playing the blind card.'

I haven't done it again.

Other situations where I play this card trick is when I am out with someone for a meal. Often the restaurant is busy with only booking reservations available. Time to put on my theatrical cap and let the light shine on me!

I will tell whoever is with me to stand back and let me take the lead. Time to hit the stage floor.

'I was hoping to get a table for two and my dog of course,' comes my feeble and insecure request. The server asks if I have a booking and I reply no. I bend down to Rhian and pat her, reassuring her that she can lie down soon and have a rest, obvious enough for the server to hear. Doing a scan over the restaurant area she tells me to wait a minute while she clears and rearranges a table for us.

Brilliant! Yes, I've done it again. Gees, I'm good. I always knew I enjoyed performing in front of people! My friend asks me if we can get in or not and I turn around and tell her the server is getting a table ready for us now. Quietly impressed, we remain subdued, to not give this act away.

Server returning, pleased to have been able to find us a table to sit at, even offers the dog a bowl of water. I tell her that Rhian would appreciate that and thank her very much for all her help. Sitting down, ready to go through the menu, my girlfriend smiles and giggles saying, 'Good on you Coll, I'll take you anywhere!' She also mentions there is a whole queue of people waiting for a table and here we are sitting down ahead of them. Now, that is playing a hand of aces in the blind card game.

The only issue I have now is I have given my game away and everyone out there will now know it. I think I will still give the performance a go just in case they haven't read about it, and don't you dare go telling them either! Weighing up the scales of Lady Justice though, I don't know why I feel so guilty. I mean, all I really gained out of it was two free coffees. It's not like I swindled money from a Swiss bank account!

I must confess, I do feel as if I have just had a sole-lifting and cathartic release, having told you about my sins. Thank you, my priestly friends, for listening to my confession.

Who is the patient?

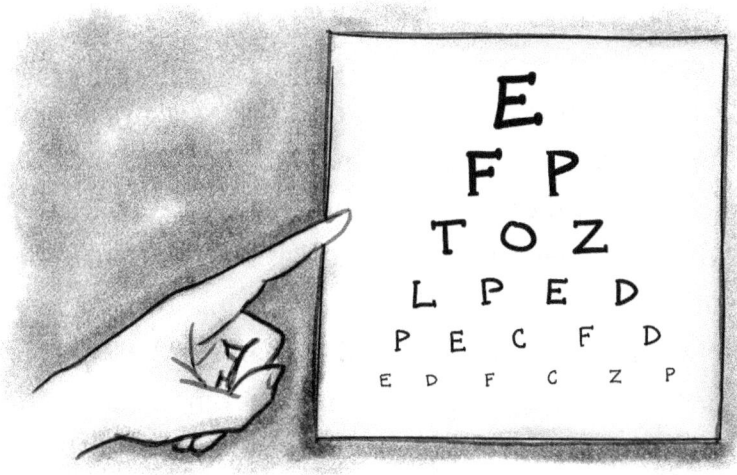

My return to work was all set in motion with the last step of the process to be finalised. I needed to get a medical clearance from the Education Department's doctor to get the all clear to work in the school. After making this appointment, a colleague from work drove me there and went in with me. I walked in with my bright hot pink cane, the medical interview set to go for launch.

Going through, it was obvious that only parts of my medical information had been sent to the doctor. He asked about the heart transplant, perhaps thinking this was the main issue for my return to work. I explained to him that everything was going along fine with my heart, and I told him about the amount of exercise and training I had been doing, and he realised my heart was not the issue. He then read on and noticed I had type one diabetes. He tried to make out like this would be an issue for my return to work, with concerns of blood sugar control and how I managed it. I told him I had lived with diabetes since I was nine and it was not an issue to be concerned with.

Reading on further, he came to the section stating I was legally blind. Hooray! Now we might be getting somewhere in that ballpark area needing some support, I thought. Now, you must realise there was a whole pile of evidence from the ophthalmologist verifying my lack of vision, clearly a no-brainer as far as I was concerned. With this information, the wise and brilliant doctor asked me if I could read any of the letters on the eye chart on the door. Really! You're kidding me, aren't you? My friend sitting with me looked bewildered. I told the doctor no, I couldn't read any of the chart, so he then asked if I could see any of it at all. I said I could see a white rectangle shape on the door. He seemed shocked and puzzled.

Holding up a pen in front of me, he asked could I see it? 'No,' was my simple response. Now for something different, he held up a different coloured pen, and brainlessly asked me the same question. Much to his surprise, I again answered no. Now, I was really beginning to wonder how in the hell did this doctor even pass his medical exam? Maybe he bought a fake one online, was my conclusion to this circus going on here!

'Let's try something completely different,' was his next stunningly intellectual brainwave. 'How many fingers am I holding up?'

'I don't know, I can't see them,' I retorted back, now getting a little frustrated with this imbecile. Still holding his hand up, he asked me to tell him when I could see it. Silence for a few seconds, then I announced, 'Now,' as his hand came out to my right side's peripheral vision. Finally concluding that I was legally blind, he seemed astonished with his findings!

He inquired what my role entailed at work, and I went through my normal tasks of scribing, reading, and helping children with low literacy levels to do their work. Baffled as to how I was going to be able to do this, he actually went on and asked exactly that. 'How are you going to read or write?' 'I don't know?' I simply replied.

'How do you use a computer?' was his next inspiring query.

'I haven't learned how to do that yet,' I answered.

'Well, how then are you going to manage back at school doing these tasks?' was his brilliantly profound question. As you can imagine, by now I was completely bemused with the questioning one would expect from a buffoon. I wanted to grab my folded-up cane, which would nicely suffice as a baton and hit him across the head to try knock some sense into him! Here comes that eruption of frustration, about to spurt out with great force and destroy everything in its path.

'You're asking me to think outside the box of sight when I have lived my whole life in that box with vision. Now to expect me to produce ideas and ways of how I am going to do things is simply ridiculous. I have no idea how I am going to do them. That is your job. You are the one that is meant to come up with the ideas of how I am going to be able to do these tasks and that's the whole reason why I have come here. You are meant to arrange help and support for my return to work. I am still living in the box of doing things with sight!' was my wrath upon him.

Now that I had put the ball back in his court of responsibility and supposedly his speciality in getting staff back to work, an awkward silence fell on us all. He then asked who my main support at home had been regarding vision issues. I told him Vision Australia had been. His quick and relieved announcement was, 'Well, then, we will get Vision Australia to implement the returning to work support process.' Completely gobsmacked with his passing the buck, as one would say, I queried if he had never before processed someone blind returning to work. His simple response was 'No.' I was the first staff member to lose sight and needed assistance in having support set in place.

I am not trying to belittle this doctor, but really! Anyone with a bit of common sense would be able to read the obvious findings, surely? Situations like this really do my head in, as I am sure it would you too?

Colleen Ashby

Lost in space... no, the bus port

I don't know if you grew up watching *Lost in Space,* or if maybe you've seen the new Netflix version? I loved both, especially the old black-and-white series with Robot rolling along following Will, suddenly erupting in this deep robotic voice: 'Warning, warning, Will Robinson. Danger approaching!' With his concertina arms flapping up and down wildly. Each week, a new adventure of being lost on some obscure planet. Following the family as they tried to navigate their new surroundings, discovering unforeseen hostile beings. Always on their mission to find their way back home to planet Earth. Well, my adventure was nowhere as exciting as Outer Space but an adventure all the same.

I began my launch on the bus. Destination: the Elizabeth Quay bus port in Perth. Navigation systems all set, as I had previously done two days of orientation training with the dog instructor, a few weeks prior to launch date. Practicing where

Ya Gotta Laugh

I got off at the terminal and where to proceed from there to navigate my way down to where I would be doing a cooking class. Confident and ready to begin my mission, Rhian and I entered the vessel for transportation. We were both excited for what lay ahead on our new challenge.

The first communication from Ground Control to Major Tom was when the captain of the ship (well, actually the bus), asked me where I needed to get off. I told him the bus port, and that the usual terminal was D. He told me he could drop me anywhere. I countered back that I would then have to find my way to C terminal to catch the blue CAT bus, and he helpfully told me he would let me off at C depot. This was to be the initial glitch in my inbuilt navigation system in my head.

Disembarking from the bus, I took my first steps of my adventure into the unknown. 'Houston, we have a problem.' This occurred when the driver dropped me right in front of the lift. I had never used the lift before, so not wanting to show the driver I didn't appreciate his help, I went to push the button. I only saw this big bright red button, so I went ahead and pressed it. Alarms and ringing tones now coming out from the speakers made the driver jump out of his bus and quickly come over to assist me. Both of us flabbergasted by the commotion of sounds going on, a voice called out. The driver told them it was a false alarm and that there was a blind lady with a guide dog coming up. Lift doors eventually opening, I thanked the driver for his help.

As I arrived on the upper concourse, I tried to gather my surroundings. I had come onto this planet on the opposite side from where I had my previous landing, and I was slightly disoriented. I worked out in my head that I was coming from the opposite direction and went straight back down the stairs I had just come up. Feeling I was now back on track, I promptly went to where the blue CAT bus would be. However, deciding to walk instead, I continued walking straight along the depot pathway. I came across a big locked yellow iron gate. I rattled it but there was no way of opening it. Then Robot's alarm warning of danger went off in my head. Hearing and glimpsing the big buses revving up and pulling out of the depot made me remember what the instructor had mentioned to me. 'You can't walk out from this level as this is where all the buses leave from, and you could get run over.' Not wanting the news headlines of the day to be 'Blind person and guide dog killed by bus,' I did a quick turnabout and marched back to where I began.

At the top of the same set of stairs I had been on only minutes earlier, I knew I had to exit the concourse at this top level. Outside and making my way, the surroundings felt unfamiliar and glimpses of trees I hadn't seen before were now in my vicinity. I was getting confused, as I had no idea where I was. Stopping and trying to look around, a passer-by asked me if I needed help. I told him I needed to get to Elizabeth Quay. He told me I was heading in the opposite direction. Turn around 180 degrees and go to the bus port. I told him that was where I had just come from. He directed me down to where I had to go.

Bewilderment to say the least had filled my head and I felt like I was Alice in Wonderland, having gone down the rabbit hole to a weird and strange world, where everything is topsy turvy. Once again up in the concourse, I think the other end but can't really guarantee that, I stood there trying to work out where the hell I was!

Then a police officer asked me if I was all right. I told him I was lost and trying to find my way down to Elizabeth Quay, he laughed and told me he thought I was. He had watched me as I popped out of the stairs, only to go back down. Then reappeared out of the same place. Watching me walk out of the bus port one end and now reappear the other. This must have been very comical for someone to observe. He told me he would walk with me however far I needed him to.

I was much relieved to have an officer of the law escort me, and we chatted all the while, which was certainly very reassuring indeed.

Now I was out of that damn bus port and back on familiar terra firma. Proceeding with confidence once more in both Rhian's and my stride, trajectory set for arrival. There was construction work ahead which was all encountered in my orientation training, so I knew I was on track. Suddenly there were large, bright barricades ahead, blocking my way.

Asking Rhian to find a way, she led me out to go around, only to discover that the barricade went all the way out to the main busy road. Robot's alarms shouted at me once more to prevent me from getting run over. About turn and following the bright blocks all the way down a side street until they ended, then I had to stop and recalibrate my navigating system.

I eventually found my way to the cooking course and told them about the relentless events disorientating me at every step of my journey. At the end of the day, I decided to just catch the blue CAT bus instead of trying to manoeuvre all those obstacles again. I was once again back in the bus port. Walking up and down the terminal, I heard the same police officer shout out to ask if I was okay.

As he came up to me I told him I needed D depot. He announced that I was in the correct place. It didn't seem familiar to me. The seats were different, and it just felt wrong. I wasn't going to dispute this helpful officer of the law, however, so I sat and waited for the time to come when I would go downstairs to catch my bus.

When I was about to embark on my ride back home, I asked the driver if this was the 282. He announced that my bus was three stops up ahead. Now at least I knew why things never felt familiar upstairs, I was on the wrong section of D. Just then I heard, 'Mrs Ashby, it's Joel from school.' Joel told the driver he would escort me up to my bus. I thanked Joel for rescuing me from getting on the wrong bus or missing my bus and having to wait another hour for the next one to come along. He told me, normally if he sees someone from school, he doesn't interact with them, but he recognised Rhian and myself and couldn't let me get lost. How lucky was I, for this lovely ex-student to help me like that?

So, as you can see, my mission was nowhere as exciting as being lost in space with alien creatures endangering my life, but still a very funny story all the same. Doing pop-outs from staircases, exiting the building one end only to reappear at the other minutes later. Getting lost on every step of my journey throughout the entire day. A police officer coming to my rescue both in the morning and afternoon, and then Joel preventing me from missing my bus. Hopefully, next week when I blast off again, I will navigate a smooth landing and stay on course the entire day!

Colleen Ashby

Book launch

March 20th 2021 was a day that will stay in my memory for the rest of my life. The fruition of completing my first book, *I Can See Clearly Now,* and time for the big reveal with an amazing book launch. Always one to do things in style and to the best of my ability, I planned it at the Harry Perkins Medical Centre, which I thought fitting as it was a heart transplant that opened my life in ways I could never have expected.

After a near catastrophic mistake, with a misunderstanding as to which hospital the Harry Perkins Centre was at, we managed to set some swift and quick-thinking plans in motion with only two days to spare. Talk about the eleventh hour. Now I know what it feels like and don't particularly want to experience it again! Luckily, as the saying goes, 'I love it when a plan comes together.' And I must say, it came together smoothly.

The sound of bustling people filled the auditorium, the guests' excited chatter heightening in volume. Music played as I walked in with Rhian by my side. It was quite overwhelming as applause began.

Chris Thomas, CEO of Transplant Australia, flew over to launch my book along with Ron Hooten, CEO of Vision Australia, who dropped in via a Zoom link from Melbourne. The next hour went by in a flash, with three songs from my book sung by a live performer throughout the talks. A Q and A with myself and Claudette Pope, owner of Footprints Publishing, was met with a lot of belly laughs at the answers I gave. Everyone in the auditorium experienced a genuine feeling of love, as other transplant recipients, friends and family all understood what the immense impact of a second chance of life meant.

Words from medical staff had people inspired and in tears at the same time, as the magnitude of challenges met along my journey was revealed. The general feedback from people was that one minute they were crying, then the next was filled with laughter. What a perfect blend of emotions.

Up there on stage, I was in my element. Engaging with the audience, entertaining them with anecdotes of humorous encounters I have had along the way with no sight. I knew that was always my joy and passion, inspiring people and having a laugh with them at the same time.

Time to sign some books. Sitting down at the table, the buzz and crowd hovering around me was incredibly hard to take in, especially as I have only a fraction of my sight. I felt like a famous movie star as people not only waited in line to have a signature but also simply to say hello, and some wanted photos taken with me.

Now I understand how fame can be intoxicating and give you a high that takes days to come down from! I was on cloud nine for at least three days after and had a buzz in me that couldn't be dulled. The feeling I experienced that day, of knowing this was my true passion and living in my heart space of boundless energy, is a memory I often use to recall joy and love when meditating. I felt vibrant and alive and knew then I was definitely on my soul's true path.

Ya Gotta Laugh

Don't drop the lead

Les and I decided to have a little getaway in Fremantle. I think the new and trendy word for this now is 'staycation.' To me it is simply a getaway. Less than an hours' drive, but a change from home. So off we went to Freo by the seaside to have a change of pace and scenery.

The hotel was directly across a large, beautiful park with tall Norfolk Island pine trees scattered throughout it, with some meandering paths to walk along. On the other side of the park was the harbour with restaurants and fish and chip shops, encompassed by a wooden decked walkway. I love coming to Fremantle, as it is a wonderful place for Rhian to keep up with her skills. The reason behind this is because within a ten-minute walk, you can traverse from a bustling metropolis of markets, restaurants and shops, meander through an open park filled with people, dogs and children, and end up walking along boardwalks echoing with the sounds of people socialising and eating. And for the final destination, the seaside awaits in all its glory.

It is important when you have a working dog to keep up the training skills in as many environments as possible. Dealing with dog distractions is where you as a handler need to have control and keep the dog on task. If the distraction training level drops, you end up with a dog that won't efficiently and safely do its job. Smells, sounds, other dogs or animals such as birds need to be encountered regularly so the dog keeps up its skills. Fremantle covers nearly every type of distraction possible.

Now, just because I decide to have a holiday, doesn't mean there is a break from Rhian's normal daily routines such as feeding and toileting. When travelling anywhere, I usually need a suitcase just for her. Her food, bowls, bedding and comfort toys all need to be bought along. No different to travelling with children, really. You need to cater for their needs too.

Rhian loves our little getaways as she usually gets to have some fun as well. This time, she got to explore a dog beach we hadn't been to before. Les, Rhian and I all enjoyed spending a few hours swimming in the ocean and walking along the beach, us throwing the frisbee for Miss Rhian. A fresh water washdown afterwards keeps her clean and respectable enough to go inside a hotel.

Morning came with Rhian jumping up on my bed and licking my face. I no longer need an alarm clock, I upgraded to a Rhian clock, which is dependable and not noisy, plus there is nothing like a big slapping tongue across your face to wake you up. I also get a Chinese massage as she walks over me. It was Rhian o'clock, time to take her out to the toilet followed by a feed. Les still asleep, I took Rhian across the park to do her toileting.

With so many new smells to choose from in deciding where to do her jobs, she got quite excited in trying to make her decision, especially with the harness off but her lead on. It's a signal that she is on her free time. Dragging me around like a horse pulling a plough, she finally found her perfect spot. Great for her but not so much for me. Out of all the beautiful lush green grass to choose from, she decided to go in the wood chips and dirt! When I don't use the toilet harness, I have to place my foot close to where she is doing her jobs, so I know where to pick it up. With this in mind, there is very little difference between her jobs and brown wood chips. At least on green grass there is a chance of seeing the contrast in colour.

Trying to keep my foot near the landmine so it didn't go off and make an explosive mess everywhere, I placed her harness down on the ground so I could try and find the doggy-do-bag in my handbag. Normally, I would just have it in my hand, but holidaying is a different circumstance. While I was fossicking around in my bag, Rhian was wanting to explore the other fantastic new smells in her unfamiliar environment. I decided to place her lead on the ground and stand on it while I picked up her jobs, as it was the only way I could hope to complete the task successfully. Landmine contained and ready for safe disposal, I picked up her lead and clipped it back together. I felt some sticky substance on the lead, so I carefully smelled my hands. Yep, that distinct disgusting smell of dog poop wafted up my nose, and it wasn't pleasant! Left hand contaminated, I still had to put on her harness with as little fallout from the mine explosion as possible. Skilfully, with my right hand I managed to buckle up her harness. Great, now how am I going to grab hold of the handle without smearing dog poop all over it? Answer is, I'm not!

Taking hold of the harness handle and the sticky poop-smeared lead, I picked up the poop bag in my right hand to find a bin. The smell of dog poo wafting all around me was not an enjoyable state to be in. I couldn't go back to the hotel like this, so I had to find a toilet to clean up in. Remembering where one was, I headed Rhian in that direction. Luckily, the cleaners were there preparing them for the day.

I did not know which type of toilet I was entering and I didn't really care with the stinking state I was in. I found my way to the wash basins, washed my hands with soap first, then took her lead off. I found some toilet paper and wet it with some added soap. I ran it along the length of the lead, using a clean side each time. The same for the handle. I used a great wad of toilet paper, but I didn't care. I wanted to get rid of the sticky stench that has a way of just lingering on.

Eventually making my way back to the hotel room, with sleeping beauty still snoozing in dreamland, I was a little more than peeved about this whole event. I wanted to vent off and blame Les for not being there to help me. Knowing he had nothing to do with it at all, I somehow managed to contain my frustration with this whole stinking mess. Going into the bathroom and grabbing some flannels, I once again soaped them up with warm water and wiped over everything again.

When I relayed the scenario back to Les, he found it quite amusing, then offered to check out the lead and harness to make sure it was clean before going down to breakfast together. Even a slight lingering odour of this type would be enough to turn anyone off their food. Not only that but nearby people would be wondering where it was coming from. I for one didn't want people thinking, 'Oh, that poor blind woman doesn't even realise she needs to change her underwear.'

The following morning, when I had to repeat the process again, I remembered a golden rule I learned when I had horses. 'No matter what, don't let go of the reins.' Well, I am changing it slightly to 'don't let go of the lead!'

Conclusion

Parting ways

I have been open, honest and insightful for you in regards to life with no sight and I hope I have shown you the trials and tribulations I have encountered along the way adjusting to my new world of becoming legally blind. Actually, that could be a great movie. Legally blind instead of blonde. It could still be a comedy. What do you think?

When I woke up blind, I knew my life would change but I didn't want everyone else's life around me to have to change because of me. With this as my driving factor, I made it my mission to keep moving forward in life to the best of my ability.

I never wanted my blindness to define or set limitations on me. I didn't want my external world to treat me any differently to how they had before. To me, I was still the same old person

I had always been. I was on a mission to prove to the world I could do anything any other person can do, if not better. The driving force within me kept pushing me relentlessly to keep trying.

I grabbed life by the horns and took back as much control as I could, never allowing it to limit or make me miss out on anything. Even though frustration and patience (or lack thereof, as it has never been one of my virtues), has gotten the better of me on many a time. I have always tried to keep a humorous and light approach to my new challenges. If I wanted to keep my family and friends on board with me, I needed to make it an enjoyable ride for all of us. I think everyone, not just me, needs to be able to laugh at themselves. See the funny side and make a joke out of it, otherwise life just becomes miserable.

I will admit I have indeed had my moments when life began to get me down, and I was thinking this was all too hard, but I knew if I stayed in that state of mind, it would soon become my way of life. It's okay to visit feeling down for a while and have a cup of tea, just don't make it your home.

I have at last come to terms with the fact there are limitations, and some things will never be the same again, which I was initially determined to prove otherwise. I was fighting against life changing, for both myself and my family, but that is not life. Life is constantly changing and evolving or else there is inertia and stagnation. Nothing in life can ever reach its full potential unless there is constant growth, support and a strive for expansion. For my boys, the gift of resilience and adaptability was theirs to have.

What I have come to comfortably resign myself to is that other doors have opened for me to step inside and see what new things await through there. People do treat me differently but now my understanding of that is, it is their own insecurities or belief systems triggering their behaviour. I am okay with that, as we are all journeying this lifetime together but have different lessons to learn. There is no right or wrong, only our perception.

Losing sight has made me stronger, more determined and opened life in a whole new way. I have been welcomed into a deeper spiritual world through yoga and meditation, which I had previously never tried. Once I let go of trying to prove to everyone that I could still do the same old things that I did before, I experienced brand new opportunities I never had before.

Writing my first book *I Can See Clearly Now*, about my life's story to that point, was something I had never dreamed of doing. Even the idea of writing a book was so far out of left field, I wouldn't have done it in a million years. Now, here I am completing my second book. If I had still had my sight, would I have written these books? I doubt it very much. It has only been through this amazing roller coaster ride in life over the past five years that I have come to this point. Life would have kept rolling on its merry old ways and patterns, and more to the point, I would say, in a rut. Staying forever in the limiting and safe space of the same old, same old. Not now.

I feel my life has been enriched and transformed in ways I could never have imagined. Through having to learn new skills, ways of getting around and getting out of my comfort zone, life has opened up beautifully for me. I spoke at a meeting one day and told the attendees if someone offered to wave a magic wand at me to give me back my sight, I would say no. I prefer the way I view life now and don't want to lose it. I have been awakened to the beauty and compassion in people. A more open and spiritual connectiveness within myself and Mother Earth. I have come to understand and discover things about myself I most probably wouldn't have done before.

When I received my selfless and cherished gift of a new heart, then through this process lost my sight, I was given not only a second chance at life but also a new way of living it. Blindness has been a gift and I have been honoured to slowly unwrap it and find its hidden gems, living life in a fuller and richer way. I honestly see it as a blessing and am profoundly grateful for both my new heart and losing my sight.

So, my fellow travellers, remember my words of wisdom: 'When you lose sight of where you are going in life, ya gotta laugh!'

Acknowledgements

I would like to acknowledge Claudette Pope, editor and owner of Footprints Publishing, for enabling my story to be heard. Once again it was a pure delight having Claudette support and guide me in producing this book, making it a reality. Light-hearted in nature with genuine regard in helping my dream come true again, I have enjoyed the laughter, love and friendship that has grown between us. I know Claudette always has my best interests at heart and will always trust her, putting any future endeavours to her to be made real. Thank you, Claudette.

I would like to give a very special and sincere thank you to Zoë Hoffman. When Claudette told me she knew an artisically talented young woman, I had no idea just how talented Zoë actually was. Giving Zoë creative freedom with the idea of doing simple sketches for each chapter title and then later on my ideas for the style of book cover I was wanting, we quickly produced amazing professional drawings. She has also produced a far more creative cover encapsulating the exact feel of what I wanted to be expressed. She has done it in such a unique and innovative way with her fresh sense of creativity. You truly are gifted and talented in your field, Zoë, and along with your beautiful personality will go far in life. Of that I am absolutely sure.

Thank you Derek Martin, the photoshoot was a lot of fun, we achieved what we wanted and I now have so many great photos to play with. Love your work.

About the Author

In March last year, Colleen Ashby had her first book published, she said there wouldn't be any others! *I Can See Clearly Now* is her memoir, *Ya Gotta Laugh* is also about her life as it is now but told in a rather different way.

A wife, mother daughter, sister; Colleen is an inspiration to many because of her zest for life, her 'can do' attitude, her willingness to learn and the love of life she shares with us.

A former high school special-needs educational assistant and fitness instructor; Colleen's next journey includes her blog 'Peacock Tales' which is a resource for those who can feel challenged by life, their health and sometimes by their mind.

Colleen is also available as a motivational speaker. To know more, visit her website - www.colleenashby.com

www.ingramcontent.com/pod-product-compliance
Lightning Source LLC
Chambersburg PA
CBHW072339300426
44109CB00044B/2089